# CONTENTS

## Chapter 20: Three-Quarter Wedge
### THANKS

# CHAPTER 1: THE "RED ZONE"

I n football, a team expects to score at least a field goal when it reaches the "red zone," the area inside the opponent's 20-yard line. Golf's red zone extends to 100 yards from the hole, but the concept is similar. When you reach this range, you must take advantage of the opportunity.

Professional golfers are, well, pros when it comes to getting up and down from 100 yards and in. They're able to control not only the distance of their shots but the spin and trajectory as well.

You may never reach tour-level proficiency in the red zone, but you can knock several strokes from your average score by honing in on these keys:

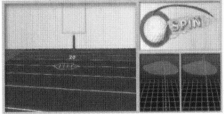

**Carry at least three wedges:** Most golfers carry a pitching wedge, which features 47° - 50° of loft, and a sand wedge with 56°. A lob wedge (60° - 64°) is a great weapon when you need to hit very high shots over hazards and stop the ball quickly on the green. Consider adding a gap wedge (51° - 53°), which will eliminate the need to hit tricky half- and three-quarter shots from yardages between your pitching and sand wedges.

**Use a ball with sufficient spin:** Pros play golf balls with the highest spin rates, though these aren't necessarily the best choice for amateurs. If you want better control around the greens without losing much (if any) distance off the tee, look for balls with urethane covers and two- or three-piece construction. They'll fly plenty far but tend to stop more quickly on the greens than surlyn or ionomer-covered balls.

**Learn different shots:** You need to be versatile to score from close range. That means learning to hit the ball high when you need to land it on a small section of green, and low when the situation calls for a running shot. Ball position is the key to altering your trajectory. Follow these basic rules:

To hit the ball high, play it nearer your left (lead) foot.

To hit it low, play the ball in the center or just right of center in your stance.

A small change in ball position can make a notable difference in flight. Experiment on the range to get a feel for this nuance.

**Play smart:** No matter how much you practice or play, you'll inevitably face challenges you can't conquer – and you shouldn't try to. Let say you've got a 50-yard shot to a flagstick cut just a few paces behind a deep bunker. To get it close, you'll have to hit a high, delicate shot that lands in the perfect spot. Miss short and you're in trouble.

The smart play is to purposely hit the ball past the pin or to aim away from the bunker. You probably won't get up and down, but you won't cost yourself strokes, either.

Few amateur golfers devote enough time or focus to the red zone, even though 60-80% of all shots (including putts) occur there. Dedicate yourself to improving in this area and you'll be way ahead of the game.

## How to Score Inside Golf's Red Zone

If you are a football fan, you are already familiar with the term 'red zone'. In the football world, this term applies when the offensive team has the ball inside the 20-yard line. When a team is 20-yards or less from the end zone, they certainly hope to score – ideally a touchdown, but at least a field goal.

Often, the game is decided by which team is better able to execute their game plan within the red zone. Scoring touchdowns instead of field goals can easily be the difference in winning or losing.

In golf, the red zone is a bit bigger, but the idea is the same. For the purposes of this chapter, we are going to consider the red zone to be any location within 100-yards of the hole. Once you are inside 100 yards, your goal should always be the same – to get the ball down in two shots.

You aren't going to always be able to pull that off, of course, but it is a great goal. By trying to get down in two, you can make your share of great par saves, and a few birdies along the way as well.

It is one thing to say that you are going to focus on scoring inside the golf red zone, but it is another thing to make it happen. In this chapter, we are going to address a number of different parts of your game that are going to contribute to your red zone performance.

It isn't just one skill which will allow you to play well from 100-yards and in. You need to be able to hit solid wedge shots, accurate chips, consistent putts, and more. Only when you have a well-rounded 'tool kit' throughout your short game will you be able to lower your scores in the red zone.

You won't be surprised to learn that you are actually going to need to practice your short game if you want to improve in this area. We say 'actually' because so many amateur golfers simply ignore this part of the game during practice.

No matter how much you like to hit drivers while standing on the range, you still need to spend plenty of time working on things like wedges and putting as well. As a good rule of thumb, try to divide up your practice time evenly between the long game and the short game.

Spend half of your time working on your full swing, and half of your time working on elements of the short game. Sticking with this plan over the long run is very likely to yield excellent results.

All of the content below is written from the perspective of a right-handed golfer. If you happen to play left-handed, please take a moment to reverse the directions as necessary.

## Putting is the Foundation

In golf, everything starts with putting. Whether you are talking about your performance in the red zone or just your game as a whole, you aren't going to make any progress without a reliable putting stroke. Although it would seem on the surface like putting should be the easiest part of the game – you are only rolling the ball along the ground, instead of sending it way up into the sky – any experienced player knows just how difficult putting can be.

Why is putting so important? It all comes down to math. Let's imagine that you play an 18-hole round and you finish with a score of 85. Not bad – but you would like to do a little bit better. Where can you find savings during such a round? Most likely, the easiest savings to find will be on the greens.

You may have had 30-or-so putts within that round, meaning you have room to trim down your total number of putts, and your overall score as a result. You can't get rid of any of your tee shots or approach shots – they are required – but you can get rid of some of your putts through improved performance.

So now that we understand why it is that putting is so critical to your score, the next step is to figure out how to improve. The points listed below will start you in the right direction.

**Practice, practice, practice.** Plenty of practice is going to be required if you are going to actually make progress on the greens. That might sound like an obvious statement, but it is one that is overlooked by a great number of players. The typical golfer wanders out onto the driving range for a practice session without even stopping to look at the putting green. After hitting a large bucket of balls, that same player walks back to his or her car and drives away.

Sure, this golfer will improve slightly thanks to working on the full swing, but some of that time could have been better spent on and around the practice green. You need a well-rounded game to shoot low scores, so plan your practice sessions to include time for both long and short game concerns.

**Master your distance control.** It is easy to fall in love with the line when you are putting. Hitting your line is important, of course, but it is only half of the equation. Good putters are not only able to hit their lines, but they are able to control distance nicely as well. We aren't just talking about lag putting here, as it is just as important to hit the ball the right speed from close range.

The line you use for a putt is always going to depend on the pace you give the ball, so having one without the other isn't going to do you any good at all. Learning to roll the ball with the right speed is going to be one of your greatest challenges as a golfer.

**Rock-solid from short range.** As it relates to scoring in the red zone, one thing you absolutely must do is make your short putts. Once you get the ball inside three feet or so from the hole, you need to be able to hole out nearly every time. All golfers will have the occasional mistake from close range, but those should be a rare exception. Most of the time, you should be burying these putts directly into the back of the cup.

If you aren't, dedicate a chunk of practice time specifically to the task of learning how to make more short putts. To get on track in this area, focus on keeping your body stable and steady while the putter swings. Also, make sure your eyes are remaining focused on the ball throughout the stroke, rather than looking up early to see where the ball is going.

**Good golfers are good putters.** Not all good golfers are great putters, but it is impossible to be a good player without at least being solid with the flat stick. Even if you only have modest aspirations for your game, you still need to invest time and effort in learning how to putt. With putting installed as the foundation of your red zone game, you can then move on to building up the other skills necessary to score the ball successfully.

## Cover Up a Variety of Yardages

Moving on from putting, we now take a look at the wedge game.

Specifically, we are going to talk about how controlling your distances is key to scoring in the red zone. Once you get inside of 100 yards, you need to be able to dial up the right yardage within a few yards either way in order to place the ball near the target.

When you are farther back, you largely control your distances with club selection. That doesn't work from inside of 100 yards, however, as you will usually be using the same club for all shots.

For example, a shot hit from 75 yards will probably be handled with the same club as a shot hit from 85 or 90 yards. However, there is a big difference in that 10-15 yards, as that means as much as 45 feet when it comes time to putt.

Having the ability to dial up the right number on command is one of the most important skills you can develop in your game. Professional golfers excel at this skill, but the typical amateur struggles badly when trying to adjust to partial yardages.

To help you get your game on track in this category, we have listed some tips below.

**Establish full swing yardages first.** The initial step in this process is going to be determining exactly how far you can hit each of your wedges with a full swing. Unfortunately, you can't get this info on the range, because range balls simply don't perform the same as actual golf balls.

Record your wedge distances while on the course over the period of a few rounds until you can settle on some solid numbers. Of course, you should ignore any shots which are hit under extreme circumstances, such as when you are playing way up or down a hill. By figuring out exactly how far you can hit the ball with each short club, you will then be able to make adjustments more reliably.

**Have three distances with each wedge.** Most amateur golfers carry three wedges in their golf bag – a pitching wedge, a sand wedge, and a lob wedge. If you learn how to hit three different shots with each of those three clubs, you will suddenly be able to cover nine different numbers with your wedges.

With each wedge, you should be able to hit a full shot, a half shot, and a three-quarter shot. As long as you can execute those shots consistently, it will be rather easy to hit a shot that is relatively close to the right number for each situation you face.

**Alter the length of the club.** Choking down on the grip of the club is one of the best things you can do to adjust your distances. Come down an inch or two from the end of the grip to take a bit of distance off of the shot – and come down even farther to create a much shorter, lower flight.

It is hard to reliably adjust the length of your swing to produce the right distance, but it is easy to choke down the same amount over and over again. Also, you can move the ball a little farther back in your stance than normal when you want to reduce distance and lower trajectory.

We have to be honest here – it is going to take some time to learn this skill. It is not easy to alter your distances reliably in the wedge game, so you shouldn't expect to master this after just a trip or two to the practice range. You can get there, of course, but only after putting in plenty of work on your technique.

## The Strategy Element

So far, we have talked about being able to hit quality shots with your putter and your wedges. Those are vital skills, to be sure, but they aren't going to get you far without a reliable strategy. You need to think clearly at all times on the golf course, but especially when you are within 100 yards of the hole.

It is easy to make mistakes in this range, and those mistakes are usually made out of laziness. Most golfers just 'point and shoot' from inside 100 yards, assuming that they don't need to think strategically. The mistakes that come from failing to think critically on these shots will cost you in a big way.

The list below contains some of the key strategies to keep in mind when inside the red zone.

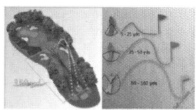

**Stay below the hole.** You could call this the 'golden rule' of red zone play. Whenever possible, you want to do what you can to keep the ball underneath the hole – in other words, you want to leave yourself with uphill shots. It is significantly easier to play uphill as compared to downhill, as the ball will stop quicker when going up a slope.

This is true both when putting and when hitting wedge shots. As you plan out your approach shot into the green, for instance, you should be thinking about how you can get close to the target while still leaving the ball on the low side.

Golf isn't always about hitting great shots. Sometimes, it is simply about placing the ball in the right spot to give yourself an easy par. Look for the low side from the first hole to the last and you will be amazed at how quickly your scores can improve.

**Avoid the short side.** This second point is nearly as important as the first. Just as you want to keep your ball below the hole whenever possible, you also want to keep the ball on the wide side of the green.

In other words, if the hole is cut on the right side of the putting surface, you want to leave your approach shot on the left. Hopefully, you will hit the green and have a birdie putt, but even if you miss, playing to the wide side will give you an easier chip. It is hard to get up-and-down when you leave your ball on the short side, especially if the short side is also the high side.

You will inevitably miss on the short side from time to time with long approach shots, but there is no reason to make such a mistake when already in the red zone. With a wedge in your hands, pick out a target that is on the wide side of the hole and execute your swing to hit your target as accurately as possible.

**Prioritize a safe result.** It is easy to become too aggressive when you get inside the red zone. For instance, if you are facing an approach shot to a hole located near a pond or deep bunker, you might fire right at it just because you only have 75-yards to the target. However, it is still possible to make a mistake on such a shot.

You could miss-hit the ball slightly, or you could misjudge the wind – and suddenly you would be faced with a difficult recovery shot or even a penalty stroke. If you are going to finish the day with a good score, you simply can't afford to waste strokes when you have red zone opportunities.

It would be great to make a birdie, but it would be a major error to card a bogey or worse. Do your best to pick targets and plan shots which give you a great chance at par while still keeping open the possibility of a birdie.

**Be aggressive when the time is right.** It is up to you to balance the last two points on this list. Yes, you want to be smart about keeping your ball in a safe position, but you also want to go for it when the course gives you a chance. On those red zone shots where there doesn't appear to be any trouble in sight, take dead aim at the target and make a great swing.

The same goes for putting. On some putts, such as long, downhill efforts, you will need to guard against being too aggressive. However, you will find some opportunities when you have a relatively short uphill putt where you can use confident speed to knock the ball into the back of the cup.

The strategy is always important in golf, no matter where on the course you happen to be standing. You always have a variety of options at your disposal for each shot, so consider them all and come to a conclusion only when you are sure that you have selected the right path. It isn't always the most talented golfer who comes out on top at the end of the day – sometimes, it is simply the golfer with the best plan.

## Know the Course Conditions

Understanding the condition of the course is important for all of your shots, but again here, this is another point that takes on extra meaning as you get closer to the green. You need to know how the ball is going to react when it lands, and you need to know how the ground is going to feel under the ball when making your swing. So which course conditions are important with regard to the red zone? Check out the following list.

**Green speeds.** You will obviously need to have an understanding of the green speeds when putting, but this information also comes in handy when you are trying to chip or pitch the ball the correct distance. Hit plenty of warm-up putts before the round starts to develop a feel for the greens that will help you once the round begins.

**The firmness of the turf.** The experience of playing golf on a dry course is dramatically different from playing on a wet one. Feel the ground beneath your feet as you walk for an idea of the turf conditions, and also watch to see how easily the turf comes out of the ground when you take a divot.

**Length of the rough.** It is important to know the length and thickness of the rough because this will affect your strategic decision making. When playing a course with difficult rough, it makes sense to play it safe and do your best to keep the ball on the short grass. However, when the rough isn't much different than the fairway, you can be aggressive and not worry if you stray a bit off the short grass.

If you want to take your scores to a new level, you are going to need to play well inside the red zone. That is easier said than done, however, so be sure to use the advice offered in this chapter to keep you on track.

# CHAPTER 2: <u>LEFT HAND OVER ROTATING</u>

O ne of the key movements essential to consistent ball striking and accuracy is the rotation of the left hand through impact.

However, if the left hand begins to over-rotate through impact, the results on ball flight can be quite dramatic. Normally, an over-rotation of the left hand will lead to shots that begin low and left of the intended target line, the greater the rotation, the more the ball will move to the left during its flight.

For golfers to hit more successful shots, it's important not to over-rotate the left hand. Here are a few ways players can practice a correct rotation.

**Slow down rotation** - At the point of impact, the back of the left hand should be pointing directly down towards the target. This helps ensure the clubface is square when it reaches the ball. To practice this position, players can practice striking through the ball, feeling the back of the left hand is pointing down the target line for as long as possible.

**Check your grip** - If a player's left hand is over-rotating it could be the cause of an overly strong grip. When the left hand becomes too strong it sits on top of the grip showing three or more knuckles when viewed from above. As the left hand comes into impact, the hand will rotate to a neutral position with the back of the hand facing the target.

This will cause a closed clubface and a shot flying off to the left. To ensure this doesn't happen, players should focus on keeping the left hand in a neutral position, this means two and a half knuckles when viewed from above with the V created by the left thumb and forefinger, pointing up towards the right shoulder.

**Ensure the hips are turning** - If the hips become inactive during the downswing, the hands can become overactive in an attempt to compensate. The hips need to turn through impact so the upper body can follow. If they don't turn through impact, the hands can 'flip' over through impact. To ensure the left hips turn through impact, ensure you finish the swing with the belt buckle facing the target.

**Don't get wristy** - If the wrists and hands become too active during the backswing they could return to impact in the same manner. Practice taking the club away with the shoulders keeping the hands, wrists, and arms connected.

## How to Stop the Left Hand Over Rotating Through Impact

The way your hands behave through the hitting area is one of the most important aspects of your swing. Of course, this part of the swing happens in just a fraction of a second, as the clubhead can easily be moving at 100 MPH or more at this time. To use your hands correctly takes not only excellent eye-hand coordination but also solid technique and plenty of practice.

Using your hands properly will help you to produce beautiful ball flights while making a mistake can lead to ugly results. Only when you refine this part of your game to allow for a consistent pattern of movement will you be able to rely on your ball flight swing after swing.

This chapter is going to deal with one specific mistake you may be making through impact – over-rotating the left hand. If you over-rotate the left hand through impact, you are likely to hit a quick hook to the left. While the slice is the ball flight that gets the most 'attention' in golf, most players would agree that a hook is actually a bigger problem.

When you hit a slice, the ball will hold up in the air and land pretty softly when it comes down. A hook, on the other hand, it a shot which is out of control. It ducks down to the ground quickly, and it usually takes a big bounce and has plenty of roll. Neither of these ball flights is desirable, of course, but you will usually be better off with a slice as compared to a hook in most cases.

As you will see as we go through this chapter, there are a number of potential causes for an overactive left hand at impact. Once you determine that this is a problem that is plaguing your game, you can get to work on finding a fix as quickly as possible.

It is hard to have much fun on the course when you continually hit quick hooks, so this is an error that needs immediate attention. Put aside other parts of your swing that you would like to work on and focus on this issue until it is solved once and for all.

There is some good news to be found if you realize that your left hand is too active through the hitting area. In most cases, this is a problem with a relatively easy solution – and once it is fixed, your swing might be in a great place.

Unlike those who hit a slice consistently, players who hook the golf ball are usually quite close to hitting good shots. With just a couple of tweaks to body positions or swing mechanics, that nasty hook just might be able to turn into a beautiful ball that soars down the fairway.

All of the content below is based on a right-handed golfer. If you play left-handed, please reverse the directions as necessary, as it will be your right hand that needs to be corrected.

## Spotting Trouble

One of the best skills you can have as a golfer is the ability to diagnose problems in your own game. You are usually all alone out there on the course in terms of trying to fix your game – even if you take lessons from a pro, he or she is typically not going to be with you when playing a round of golf. So, with that in mind, you need to develop the ability to spot problems in your game and fix them before they become bigger issues.

As it relates to the topic of this chapter, there are a few signs you can watch for which would indicate that you are over-rotating your left hand through impact. Three of those signs are listed below.

**Consistent hooks.** A pattern of shots that are hooked to the left of your target would be the biggest sign that you are allowing your left hand to over-rotate through the hitting area. It is tough to even get around the golf course when you are fighting a hook, so this is a problem that you will certainly notice as soon as it arises.

Not only will you struggle to shoot a good score while dealing with a hook, but you will also likely lose several golf balls along the way. A hook is even harder to deal with than a slice, meaning the game probably isn't going to be much fun while you work on correcting this issue. An overactive left hand is not the only potential cause of a hook, but it is almost always at least a part of the story.

**Deep divots.** If you let your left hand turn the club down too aggressively while approaching impact, you are likely to stick the clubhead way down into the turf. As a result, you are going to pull a big chunk of turf out of the ground, and you shot will have too much backspin on your shots as well.

While it is usually good to take a small divot on most of your iron shots, you really don't want to smash your club into the ground time after time. If you can manage to reduce the amount of left-hand action you are using through the ball, your divots should shallow out and your ball striking should improve as a result.

**Inconsistent play.** All golfers complain about their inconsistency, but those who have their games move dramatically up and down from round to round may be using too much hand action through the ball.

It is hard to time your hand rotation properly at impact, meaning you have to be in a perfect rhythm from your entire round if you want to succeed this way. Taking some of that hand action out of the swing is going to make you significantly more consistent, as your body rotation is far easier to time properly as compared to hand rotation.
If your scores vary wildly from day to day, it will be worth looking into the possibility that you have too much left-hand rotation in your action.

**Poor play around the greens.** You can actually use your performance around the greens to judge the way you are performing in the full swing. Do you struggle to make solid contact with your chip shots? If so, it may be that you are using too much hand action in your full swing – and that excess action could be carrying over into your short game.

While it is okay to use a little bit of hand action around the greens, you don't want to have your chipping motion made up of all hands and wrists. By stabilizing the way you swing the golf club on full shots, your chipping motion should come together nicely as well.

You should never ignore signs of trouble in your golf game. No matter what those signs may be indicating, it is always wise to address them as soon as possible. Instead of just hoping your game will fix itself on its own – which isn't going to happen – you can be proactive and take matters into your own hands. With regard to over-rotating your left hand, watch for the issues above, and get down to work on the necessary corrections once the problem has been identified.

## The Role of Your Grip

The way your hands and wrists work as the club moves through impact is going to have a lot to do with how you hold the club during the swing. It is common for amateur golfers to ignore the technical side of their grip, instead of focusing on other parts of the swing.

This is a mistake, of course, as your grip is one of the biggest fundamentals in the game. Get your grip right, and everything else gets easier. In fact, if you can get your grip right, you just might find that your excessive left-hand rotation solves itself without any other steps being required.

If you decide to improve on your grip as a way to improve your swing overall, you need to know that you are in for a significant amount of work. Grip changes are notoriously difficult to complete, as you are going to be changing the entire way your hands interact with the club.

However, while it is going to be tough, it can be extremely rewarding as well. There is the possibility that a grip change will take your game to a new level – and that should be enough motivation for you to see this through from start to finish.

When you are ready to get down to work on your grip, make sure you keep track of the following points.

**Set your left hand in a strong position.** The vast majority of amateur golfers are going to be served well by using a strong left-hand grip. It is possible to play well with a weak grip too, of course, but that is usually a more difficult path. Also, that style of grip is going to require plenty of hand action through the ball, and hand action is exactly what we are trying to avoid here.

When you look down at your left hand from address, you should be able to see at least two of the knuckles on the back of your left hand, if not more.

Many golfers play well while looking at three knuckles at address, although you probably want to stop before you get to the point of seeing all four.

**Match your right hand to your left.** You should always place your left hand on the grip prior to your right. Once your left hand is in place, add the right hand by matching it up to the position of your left. In other words, your palms should be facing each other perfectly when the grip is completed.

One of the common grip mistakes made by amateurs is having the two hands working against each other. If your hands are going to work properly through the hitting area, they need to be perfectly coordinated from start to finish. Make sure your right-hand matches up with your left as the grip is formed and you will be a big step closer to using your hands correctly.

**Modest grip pressure.** It is easy to make the mistake of squeezing tightly onto the grip when you address the ball. A tight grip is a problem because it puts too much of the control of the movement of the club into your hands and fingers.

You would rather control the club with your big muscles because those muscles are more predictable and easier to manage. You don't need a particularly tight grip to maintain control during the swing, so practice using light grip pressure to allow your hands to work more effectively.

If you are having trouble getting comfortable with a light grip, practice on some short shots before working your way up to full swings. You never want to lose control of the club as you swing, of course, so find a happy medium where you have control and yet still have the freedom you need.

**A snug connection.** You are free to decide how you would like to connect your two hands during the swing – but you do need to make sure they are properly connected. Many amateur golfers choose the interlocking grip because it firmly connects the right hand to the left, but the overlapping grip has plenty of supporters as well. Experiment with different options until you decide which grip gives you the best results overall.

It probably won't be very exciting to work on your grip for an extended period of time, but you need to stick with it if you are going to have big improvements come your way in the end. A solid grip is something that can give you confidence as you head around the course, and you can never have enough confidence in this game.

## Body Rotation is Key

Once you are sure that you have a solid grip working for you, the next step is to check on the body rotation you are using through the ball. Your body rotation is the biggest element of the downswing, and a good turn will make it very unlikely that your left hand will rotate too aggressively at impact. The combination of great grip technique and an aggressive body turn will virtually eliminate any chance of your left hand rolling over at the bottom of the swing.

To give yourself a good chance of rotating properly in the downswing, the first thing you should do is start with hip action immediately from the top. Don't bring your arms down first and then try to catch up with your hips later – it needs to be the hips which start the turn toward the target. When your hips get out in front and lead the way for your golf swing, it will naturally become easier to deliver a controlled, powerful blow into the back of the ball.

Assuming you do get the downswing off to a good start, you can't just rest on the fact that everything else will take care of itself. The swing can still go wrong, and you need to remain focused and work hard to ensure that you get through the rest of the motion properly. The biggest potential risk is giving up on your rotation and letting it come to a stop before the shot has been sent on its way.

This is an error that is made by countless amateur golfers, and it is one that may encourage your left hand to roll over. As the club is approaching impact, don't let up at all – keep turning hard toward the target and trust that the ball is going to take off in the right direction once it is struck.

The golfer who makes a great turn – both back and through – is going to be in an excellent position to hit quality shots. If you ever watch golf on TV, you will notice that professional golfers always use a powerful turn, and you should be doing the same. You can't build enough speed with your arms alone if you want to hit long, solid shots toward your targets.

Also, the swing you make with your arms and hands is never going to be as consistent as the one you make with your body. Focus some of your upcoming practice sessions on quality body rotation and you can be sure your game will move in the right direction.

## Hand Action in the Short Game

We touched briefly on the topic of the short game earlier, but it deserves a bigger mention here because your hand action is important when playing on and around the greens as well. You aren't going to shoot low scores if you struggle with the short game, so this area of your technique deserves just as much attention as your full swing.

Right off the bat, we can eliminate the putting stroke as a point of concern with regard to hand action. Why? Simple – there should be no hand action in the putting stroke. Your putting stroke should be managed entirely with your shoulders and arms, while the rest of your body stays perfectly still.

If you do allow your hands to move while trying to roll the ball toward the hole, it is likely that the club will be twisted off of the intended target line. Also, it will be difficult to control your speed when your hands are too active. Take all hand action out of your putting stroke, and work on improving your results through plenty of repetition during each practice session.

When you step off of the green, you will need to engage your hands in the action in order to chip or pitch the ball properly. This is where you have to again watch out for the mistake of over-rotating your left hand through impact. Often, this over rotation will take place when you get nervous. When the nerves kick in, you might force the action a bit, using your hands to gouge the ball out of the grass aggressively.

It is hard to control these kinds of chip shots, and you are more than likely going to miss-hit some of them as well. To avoid over-rotation, keep your left wrist firm through the ball and keep the club moving toward the target. As long as the clubhead doesn't slow down or stop during the forward swing, you should be able to strike a solid chip without much trouble.

If you find your ball in a greenside bunker and you are planning to play an 'explosion' shot to get the ball out of the sand and onto the green, you will need to plan on using an aggressive release. In this specific situation, it is okay to fully release your wrists and hands through the shot in order to cut the club through the sand successfully.

Aim for a spot in the sand a couple of inches behind the ball and swing hard. With a full release, you should be able to send the clubhead under the ball cleanly, and the shot should float up softly out of the trap and onto the green.

Over rotation with your left hand can lead to a serious problem in your game. Fortunately, most players will be able to get over this issue with a combination of an improved grip and great body rotation.

Once you fix any grip technique errors which may have been in your game, and once you learn how to turn through your shots efficiently, the quick hooks that you were likely hitting should be a thing of the past. Now that you don't have to worry about the hook, you can look forward to bigger and better things on the course.

◆ ◆ ◆

# CHAPTER 3: <u>WEDGE SHOTS:</u>
## <u>DISTANCE CONTROL</u>

W hile some golf courses and driving ranges feature excellent short game practice areas, many are woefully lacking in this critical department.

The typical facility will offer targets in 25- to 50-yard increments, starting at the 50-yard mark.

If you lack an adequate place to practice your game from 50 yards and in, there's an easy solution right in your back yard – literally. Even if the grass isn't up to golf course standards (or you'd rather not hack it to pieces), you can buy a synthetic turf mat from your local golf retailer or an online shop.

You'll need one additional prop to use as a target, such as a laundry basket or bucket. Place the target in a good spot, then mark spots at 10, 20, 30, and 40 yards from the object. (If you've only got 20 yards of space, just go to 20.)

Start by hitting 12 balls from 40 yards out, then move to the next spot, and so on. Within 15 minutes, you'll have hit four dozen practice shots. It may not sound like much, but do this

Several nights each week and you'll see a marked improvement on the course.

How and Why Practice Wedge Shot Distance Control

In golf, the wedges are often referred to as the 'scoring clubs'. That name pretty much says it all in terms of the importance of your wedges – they are critical if you hope to shoot good scores. If you think about it for a moment, it makes perfect sense that your wedges would have a strong influence over your score at the end of the day.

Hitting good wedges will set you up with short putts, and short putts are always going to be easier to make than long ones. If you can improve your skills with all of the wedges in your bag, it is almost certain that your scores will quickly come down.

Good wedge play comes down to distance control. While you obviously need to get the ball online in order to hit a good shot, doing so with a wedge is not a significant challenge. Most of your wedge shots will be online, as it is very difficult to produce a big draw or fade when a wedge is in your hands.

Knowing that you should be able to get the ball online with little trouble, your success or failure is going to come down to your ability to manage distance properly. Most professional golfers are quite adept at this task, while many amateurs struggle.

In this chapter, we are going to cover a variety of topics related to your ability to control distance on wedge shots. This might seem like a relatively narrow topic to cover with an entire chapter, but it is extremely important that you manage to improve in this area. You will notice that the rest of the game will become easier if you are able to take a step forward with your distance management.

Also, your distance control with the rest of your clubs should improve if you are able to dial in your yardages more accurately with wedges. By the end of this chapter, we hope you have all of the information you need to get out and work on this point for yourself.

Before you get started working on your distance control with the short clubs, you should take a moment to make sure you have the right collection of wedges in your bag. For most amateur golfers, carrying three wedges is going to be the way to go.

To start with, of course, you will have your pitching wedge, which is likely part of your full iron set. From there, you should have two wedges that fall into the gap/sand/lob wedge category. The exact loft on these clubs will depend on your own personal preferences, as well as the kind of courses you usually play.

It is common to have a 52* wedge along with a 58* wedge, but you could opt to go with 54* and 60* instead. If possible, experiment with different loft combinations until you settle on a set that fills all of your distance gaps nicely.

All of the content below is based on a right-handed golfer. If you happen to play left-handed, please take a moment to reverse the directions as necessary.

## The Advantages of Great Distance Control

There are a number of ways in which your game will benefit when you learn how to dial up your distance control just right with a wedge in your hands. If you currently struggle with this part of your game, making even minor improvements will open up a whole new world of possibilities to you on the course.

The list below includes a number of ways in which your game stands to be improved by simply learning how to hit your wedges the right distance time after time.

**Set up more birdie putts.** This should be the most obvious point on the list. When you wedge the ball close to the hole by controlling your distance nicely, you will frequently set up makeable birdie putts.

Of course, you aren't going to make all of those putts, but giving yourself more chances is going to result in a higher birdie total at the end of the day. As long as you are hitting enough good tee shots to give yourself wedges into the greens, you will have the enjoyable task of trying to drain as many birdie putts as possible over the course of 18 holes.

**Save par after a bad drive.** Often, when you hit a bad drive, you will find yourself facing a wedge shot after you have pitched the ball back to the fairway. These wedge shots frequently are played from between 50 – 100 yards from the green, and they are critical to your success. If you can get up and down for par from these kinds of situations, you will be able to keep your score on track.

All golfers hit bad drives from time to time, and it is the ability to get out of those holes with a par which will largely determine your overall scoring capability. Pro golfers are great at saving par after they have made a mistake, and you should be trying to take your game in that same direction.

**Avoid a big mistake.** One of the worst things you can do for your score is to dump a wedge shot into a bunker, hazard, or another penalizing place. You need to take advantage of your wedge opportunities by turning them into pars at the very least – if not birdies. Making bogeys or even double bogeys when you have a wedge into the green is a mistake that you simply can't afford to make.

If you are able to hit the ball the right distance with your wedges, you should be able to stay away from any major hazards with the majority of your wedge approaches. Even if you don't hit the ball perfectly next to the cup, at least knocking it on the green will keep you out of trouble and keep your score on track.

**Greater confidence.** Anytime you improve on your skills in one particular area of your game, you will grow your overall confidence on the course. And, as you might know, confidence is essential when trying to play good golf. You need to believe in yourself on the links, and you need to be sure that you have what it takes to move the ball around the course successfully.

Once you learn how to control your wedge distances nicely, you will have yet another reason to feel confident when you play. Even though this is only one area of a wide-ranging game, you may find that your added wedge confidence spills over into other parts of your game almost immediately.

It should go without saying that your golf game will be improved overall if you are able to control the distance of your wedge shots. If you are willing to invest some time and effort in learning how to control your distances nicely, the results should be impressive. Throughout the rest of this chapter, we are going to offer advice on how you can do just that.

## *The Basics*

There are some basic 'rules' which apply to distance control when talking about wedge shots. While you don't necessarily have to follow each of these rules, they are highly recommended. If you go against any of these basic rules in a significant manner, you will likely struggle to gain control over your distances.

Even if these concepts go against what you have previously thought about the wedge game, give them a try on the range before dismissing them altogether. Most likely, you will come to find that these tips do give you a serious advantage in terms of distance control with your short clubs.

**Keep the ball down.** This is one of the biggest points of confusion among amateur golfers. Most players think that they need to toss the ball high up into the sky when playing a wedge shot into the green. After all, your wedges have a high degree of loft, so why not use that loft to hit a high shot?

This seems like a good plan, but there is one major problem – you will lose control over the distance of the shot when you hit the ball high. While it is up in the air, the ball can be affected by the wind, and it can carry longer or shorter than expected based on launch angle, spin rate, and other factors. It is a far better plan to keep the ball close to the ground.

When you play low wedge shots, you take many of the variables out of play and you wind up with more consistent results. Thanks to the spin on the ball, you should have no trouble stopping your wedge shots quickly, even though they are taking a lower trajectory than you might have used previously. Once you get used to playing low wedge shots into the greens, you will wonder why you ever bothered trying to hit the ball so high.

**Make a compact swing.** There is simply no need to make a long, loose swing when you are holding onto a wedge. Instead, you should be making a compact move that keeps your arms close to your body throughout the motion.

There is no need to create significant speed when hitting a wedge, so you don't need to be making a long swing. In other words, your wedge swing should look nothing like your driver swing. If you can teach yourself to keep your arms close to your body as you hit wedges, your distance control will quickly become more reliable. Also, as an added benefit, you will improve your ability to achieve a clean strike when you employ this method.

**Use soft hands.** You should always have your hands relaxed while holding onto a golf club, but that point is especially important when it comes to wedge shots. If you are playing a wedge into the green and you need to control your distance perfectly, one of the best things you can do is to keep your hands relaxed and loose.

You have to hold on tight enough to keep the club in your hands, of course, but you need to avoid squeezing tightly as you swing. Soft hands will allow you to swing the club through with a smooth rhythm, and that rhythm is going to help your ability to dial up the right yardage.

**Have a specific number in mind.** This might seem like a silly tip, but it is one that many amateur golfers actually overlook. Before stepping up to hit your iron shot, you need to know exactly how far you are trying to hit the ball.

Do you need to carry the shot 80 yards, or 85? How much bounce do you expect to get after the ball lands? You need to be as specific as possible when preparing to hit the shot. Unfortunately, many players get sloppy with their yardages when they get close to the green, thinking they can judge the distance with their eyes instead of an actual measurement. Don't make that mistake.

Take a moment to get accurate yardage to the target and then keep that number in mind as you plan out your shot. Paying attention to detail in this area is going to be a big help in the battle for more accurate wedge shots.

The four points above will take you a long way toward accurate wedge shot distances. As mentioned earlier, be sure to give these points a try before you dismiss them out of hand. It is important that you work on each of the points individually as they can lead to a powerful effect when all added up.

## The Practice Challenge

You are going to run into a very specific problem when you set out to work on your wedge distance control – where do you practice this skill? While the first place that comes to mind might be the driving range, you will soon find that your local driving range is of little use in this area.

Since you are hitting range balls rather than real range balls, the distances you see on the range are irrelevant when trying to figure out how far the ball is going to travel on the course. You should never base any distance decisions for your golf game on what you see happening on the range, as those golf balls cannot be trusted.

Many of them are flight restricted, they may not have any dimples left, and the core could be battered from so many uses. Simply put, it is important to ignore all distances you see on the range.

So, if the range is out, where do you turn? You may be able to find a golf course near you with a large short game practice area where you can hit some wedge shots. Some courses offer a short game area that extends back to 50 yards or so, if not a bit farther.

That isn't going to allow you to hit full shots, but it is enough to allow you to work on your partial wedges. To find a facility with such a practice area, call around to local golf courses and ask what they offer for short game practice. With any luck, you will be able to find one or two options in your local region.

The other option is the golf course itself. As you play, be sure to write down your distances on each wedge shot you hit. You will likely hit quite a few wedges during any round, so you should quickly develop a 'book' on your own distances. If you are vigilant about writing down distances over the course of a few rounds, you will start to get a great picture of how far you hit each wedge.

Then, as you make changes to your technique and shot selection, you can note how those distances evolve. Your best learning tends to take place on the golf course anyway, so it makes sense to look to your on-course play for progress in this area.

While the driving range is not going to help you in terms of learning distances, it should still be used as a place where you can sharpen your technique. Practice hitting low wedge shots with a controlled swing over and over again on the range. Always pick a target for these kinds of shots, and pay attention to all the small details in the swing just as you would on the course.

The driving range should be about more than just launching drivers into the distance, which seems to be the only thing most players want to do when at the range. Include time for refining your wedge swing and it will be a bit easier to repeat your distances over and over again on the course.

## Reading the Bounce

One of the biggest skills you need to develop with regard to wedge play is learning how to read the bounce of the ball. You need to be able to predict how the ball is going to bounce before it has even hit the ground – which can be a challenge, to say the least.

Fortunately, this is a task that is going to get easier with experience. Once you get comfortable with the typical trajectory of your iron shots, and the course conditions in your area, you should be able to reliably guess at how far the ball is going to bounce after it lands on the green.

To give you a boost in this area, we have provided a few quick tips below.

**Pay attention before the round.** Prior to walking to the first tee, pay attention to how the ground feels below your feet during warmups. Does the ground feel hard and dry, or is there some give in the turf?

Most likely, the turf conditions around the practice area are going to closely match the conditions out on the course itself. Soft conditions are obviously going to lead to shorter bounces than firm conditions, so make note of what you find and keep that information in the back of your mind as you play.

**The trajectory is important.** A wedge shot that comes in on a low trajectory is going to take a long, flat bounce, while a higher wedge shot will bounce back up higher into the air. Think about the trajectory you plan on using for the wedge shot in front of you, and take that into consideration while trying to predict the bounce. Remember, the lie of the ball is going to influence trajectory greatly, so plan on a higher shot when you play from an upslope (and a lower shot when playing from a downslope).

**Be quick to adjust.** If you guess wrong about the bounce of the ball on the first couple of holes, don't be too stubborn to adjust your way of thinking. Use the information you have picked up from those early holes to make better decisions as the round goes on.

If the ball is bouncing farther than you expected, adjust your distances accordingly and hit the ball shorter in the air. The golfer who comes out on top at the end of the day is often the one who is willing and able to adjust on the fly. Learn from early mistakes and make yourself better as the round progresses.

The ability to dial-up accurate wedge distances is rare among the amateur golfing crowd. If you can teach yourself to excel in this area, you will certainly have a leg up on your competition at the local club.

Take the advice we have provided above and get to work on this important skill. With your wedges now flying a predictable distance, you will be a big step closer to playing the best golf of your life – and you should have more fun on the course in the process.

◆ ◆ ◆

# CHAPTER 4: <u>INTO THE WIND</u>

W hat's the worst thing you can do when playing into the wind? Hit a high left-to-right shot (a fade). For a lefty, it would be a right-to-left ball flight. A headwind exaggerates any spin your ball carries, so a fade gets pushed far off line and flies a very short distance.

The ball appears to balloon up and sideways as the wind kills its progress. A right-to-left shot, or draw, is less affected because it flies with less backspin and tends to penetrate the wind. If you're capable of hitting a draw, use it whenever possible in windy conditions.

If a draw's not in your arsenal, you can still survive windy days playing your fade – the great Lee Trevino made a career of it. The first trick is to keep the ball low, which can be difficult since the fade is hit with an open clubface. The second key is to make sure the ball starts left of your target.

**To play a fade into the wind:**

With the driver, tee the ball slightly lower than normal, with only a small portion of the ball above the club's top line.

With every club, play the ball back in your stance. A couple of inches inside the left (lead) heel for the driver, mid-stance for irons.

Aim the clubface a little left of your intended target, with the feet and body aligned with the club or just slightly left. You're looking for a minimal fade.

On the takeaway, be sure to swing the club back along the line of your body while keeping the clubhead low to the ground.

Swinging through, fire your right side through the shot. This will prevent the ball from squirting right while starting it on target and delivering the solid contact necessary to minimize the wind's effect.

Follow the same steps for shots with irons or woods from the fairway, playing the ball slightly back in your stance.

## How to Play a Fade into the Wind

It is never easy to play golf in the wind. Even the best players would rather play in calm conditions as opposed to having to deal with a breeze, as the wind is always unpredictable and difficult to judge. Golf is a game with numerous variables involved in each shot, so the last thing you need is to add another one to the mix.

However, there is nothing you can do to prevent the wind from coming up while on the course, so you need to learn how to deal with it properly. With the right plan, you can get your ball around the course without too much interference from the breeze sweeping across the course.

When you think about playing golf in the wind, you probably picture yourself hitting a bunch of low draws around the course. After all, a draw is usually the shot that most players turn to in the breeze, since it offers a lower spin rate and typically a lower flight than a fade.

But is it necessary to use a draw when the wind comes up? Not necessarily. In this chapter, we are going to look at the unique idea of playing a fade into the wind. You may do this by choice, or you may play a fade into the breeze simply because you aren't capable of producing any other ball flight.

Whatever the case, the chapter below will attempt to outline how you can hit this kind of shot with success. Even if you don't have a draw in your playbook at the moment, you still may be able to create quality scores on windy days.

Before we get into the specifics of how to play your fade in these conditions, we should talk first about the basics of playing in the wind. Playing in the wind is difficult, of course, but it is not impossible. And, since no one has yet invented an entirely indoor golf course, this is a challenge that is not going away anytime soon. To make sure you are on the right track with regard to playing your best on a windy day, keep the following basic tips in mind.

**Play with plenty of margin.** One of the first things to do when playing in the wind is to pick safer targets for all of your shots. Instead of aiming at a flag cut on the side of the green, for example, consider aiming for the middle of the putting surface.

You simply aren't going to have as much control over your ball in the wind, so don't be too aggressive with your targets. Pick shots that give you as much margin for error as possible, and then execute confident swings in order to keep the ball out of trouble.

**Take what the wind gives you.** This is the point that trips up most amateur golfers. There is nothing you can do about the wind, so you need to accept it as a reality and play within the constraints that it puts on your game. What does that mean?

Think about it this way – you are playing a different golf course on a windy day as compared to a calm day. Where you might be able to reach the green on a given par four in two shots on a calm day, that same green might be out of reach in the wind.

And that's okay – rather than trying to force your ball there in two shots, play it as a three-shot hole and hope to make your putt for par. Forcing the action in the wind is only going to lead you into trouble. It takes patience to play this way, but your score will benefit from a patient and level-headed approach in the breeze.

**Focus on your short game.** The wind will have very little if any, effect on your short game. With that in mind, you should do your best to focus on executing your short game shots perfectly on a windy day. Your approach shots aren't going to be as accurate as they would be in calm weather, so there is a good chance you will need to chip more than normal.

Spend a few extra minutes on your chipping and putting before the round starts, and plan on doing great work on and around the greens. With a strong short game performance, you just might be able to make up for the strokes that the wind tried to take away.

**Have a good attitude.** The game you play between your ears on a windy day is nearly as important as the swings you make. If you take a good attitude with you onto the course, you will stand a far better chance to post a good score.

Don't head to the first tee feeling frustrated about the wind – instead, look at it as an opportunity to play a great round in spite of the conditions. If you embrace the challenge which comes along with a windy day, your patience will improve, as will your performance.

As we move on in this chapter, we are going to shift our attention specifically to using your fade into the wind. However, keep the general tips above in mind while playing on a windy day and you will begin to perform well even in these challenging conditions.

All of the content below is based on a right-handed golfer. If you happen to play left-handed, please take a moment to reverse the directions as necessary.

## Making It Work

On the surface, it is true that it doesn't make much sense to hit a fade when playing into the wind. After all, a fade is going to fly higher than a draw in most cases, and you certainly don't want to hit the ball high when hitting a shot into the breeze.

Also, a fade will usually have a higher backspin rate than a draw, which is another strike against you. Keeping your spin rate down in windy conditions is always advised, and going with the left-to-right shot will not help you toward that end.

The first thing you need to understand about fading the ball into the wind is that you cannot swing hard at these kinds of shots. If you were to swing hard, the spin rate on the ball would increase, and the shot would climb high into the sky.

Once up in the air, the wind will kill the forward momentum of the shot, and you will almost certainly wind up short of the target. Anytime you are trying to fade the ball into the breeze, you need to make a soft swing while using plenty of club to cover the target. By avoiding the mistake of an aggressive swing, you can reduce your spin rate successfully and you should be able to keep the ball much closer to the ground as it flies.

Of course, as is the case with any shot played into the wind, you need to plan on losing yardage off of your usual number with a given club. For some reason, this is a tough lesson for some amateur golfers to accept.

Many players stubbornly continue to hit the same club they would use from given yardage, even if the wind is blowing in their face. Or, at the most, they will take one extra club. It is common for a shot affected by the wind to require two or three extra clubs, depending on the situation, and there is nothing wrong with that at all.

Don't try to impress your friends by how hard you can hit the ball into the wind – that approach will only lead to disappointing results. Especially when hitting the ball into the wind with a fade, you need to understand that at least one extra club will be needed, if not two or more.

Another piece of this puzzle is determining how far to the left to aim your shot in order to allow it to turn back toward the target. Since you are hitting into the wind, you should expect the ball to curve more as it flies.

Many players make the mistake of thinking that only a crosswind will cause the ball to move to the right or left, but that is actually not the case. When hitting into the wind, you should expect any curve on your ball to be amplified, whether it is a draw or a fade. Likewise, when hitting downwind, you will see your shots straighten out.

There is no exact way to determine how much your shots will be affected by the breeze, so you are going to have to learn this point by experience. As you hit more and more shots into the wind as time goes by, you will get better at predicting the path of the ball. As long as you are aware of this concern, you can keep it in mind while picking a target line.

Is a fade the ideal shot to hit when playing into the wind? No – not really. However, it certainly can work, as long as you understand the limitations of the shot and what you need to watch out for as you go. By making a relatively soft swing and giving the ball plenty of room to turn back to the right, you can fade the ball into the target even when the breeze is blowing in your face.

## Picking the Right Time

If you are also capable of hitting a draw on command, you will need to pick the right time to use the fade into the wind. After all, the draw would be the more conventional shot, so you will likely want to go that way the majority of the time. The list below highlights some situations when you will be better served to cut the ball into the breeze.

**Need to stop the ball quickly.** Few shots in golf will stop as quickly as a$ fade which is played into the breeze. If you move the ball from left to right while the wind blows in your face, you can expect the ball to stop almost immediately when it lands. Even in firm conditions, this is the kind of shot that shouldn't really go anywhere when it hits the turf.

If you need to stop the ball quickly, such as would be the case when playing to a front hole location, think about turning to the fade for help. As long as you pick the right club in this situation, you may be able to drop the ball right next to the cup for an easy birdie putt.

**Don't have to carry a dangerous hazard.** When you opt to go with the fade into the wind, there will always be the risk of having the ball balloon and come up short of the target. You will work to avoid that outcome by making a soft swing, but it is a possibility nonetheless.

With that in mind, it would be wise to avoid this shot when you absolutely need to carry the ball the full distance to the target. For instance, if there is a water hazard short of the green, playing your fade may be taking on too much risk.

In this situation, play a draw (if you can) or even a punch shot to avoid the wind and get the ball over the hazard. One of the biggest keys to posting low scores is simply staying away from penalty strokes – don't make a costly mistake by letting the wind drop your ball into a bad position short of a target.

**Facing a shot of more than 100 yards.** Distance plays a role in this decision-making process as well. If you are playing in from more than 100 yards, feel free to think about the idea of using a fade. From closer than 100 yards, however, leave the fade in the bag and just hit a relatively straight, low wedge shot in toward the target.

Trying to fade the ball from such a short distance is going to send the ball way too high into the air, letting the wind dramatically affect your distance control. Learn how to play the ball under the wind from these short distances and you will find yourself with short putts more often.

With practice, you will get more and more comfortable with the task of picking the right time for this shot. In addition to the points above, trust your own instincts as well. If the shot doesn't look right to you for some reason, think about going in another direction. You always have to believe in the shot you are trying to hit, so never start your swing until you are fully committed to the choice you have made.

## Use Care in Soft Conditions

Usually, soft conditions make the game of golf easier. When the ground is soft, the ball doesn't bounce or roll much after it lands – meaning you can control your shots far more precisely than you can on hard ground.

You will be able to aim directly at most of your targets, expecting the ball to land and settle down quickly. Professional golfers usually shot low scores in soft conditions, and it is common to see rounds in the low 60s when rain falls on the best players in the world.

With all of that said, you need to be careful when playing on soft conditions to avoid spinning your ball back off the green. This is true of every short approach shot you hit, but it is particularly true when hitting a fade into the wind.

Playing into the wind is going to cause your ball to fly extremely high, so it will be coming down on a steep angle when it returns to earth. When you combine that steep angle with a high spin rate, the ball can easily zip back off the green. Or, at the very least, it can spin back far enough to take you away from your intended target.

Many amateur golfers think it's 'cool' to spin the ball back on the green, as this looks like a shot that the pros would hit. Don't get caught up in that line of thinking. The shot might look cool, but it is actually quite difficult to use effectively.

Rather than spinning the ball back, your goal should be to have the ball sit still once it lands. It is far easier to leave the ball next to the hole when it sits in place than trying to judge a significant amount of backspin.

So what can you do to avoid excessive backspin? For one thing, you need to swing soft on into the wind shots, as we mentioned previously. Also, it is important to make sure that you are playing the right ball.

While it is often against the rules (if you are in a competition) to switch golf balls during a round, you can certainly pick the type of ball you are going to play before the round begins. So, if you know you will be facing soft conditions, use a ball that offers a slightly lower spin rate. This adjustment will automatically take backspin off of your approach shots, and it should make it easier to hold the putting surface.

## *Learn a Draw*

In golf, you always want to have options. As we have explained in this chapter, it is possible to hit some quality shots by using your fade into the wind. However, that is not always going to be the right play. If the only shot you can hit is a fade, you will struggle to post consistently good scores on windy days. It would be ideal to have a draw at your disposal, even if you only use it from time to time. To learn how to play a helpful right to left shot, review the points below.

**Move the ball slightly back in your stance.** Many golfers think that moving the ball back in the stance will cause them to hit shots out to the right, but the opposite is usually true. With the ball farther back, you will contact the shot while the club is still moving away from your body – creating the right to left spin that you need. Don't move the ball too far back, however, as doing so will make it difficult to strike solid shots.

**Use a strong left-hand grip.** If you usually play a fade, you might be able to turn that fade into a draw simply by turning your left hand slightly to the right on the top of the grip. This will put your hands in a stronger position, meaning they will have an easier time releasing the clubhead through impact. An improved release will lead to a closed clubface, which is going to produce a draw when all is said and done.

**Take your time.** One of the keys to hitting a draw is simply taking your time at the top of the swing. If you rush through the transition from backswing to downswing, you won't be able to stay behind the ball properly – and a fade (or slice) is the likely outcome. Take your time throughout the swing, and especially at the top, to make sure you are well-positioned to strike a clean draw.

There is no such thing as a perfect golf shot that works in all situations. The nature of this game demands that you be creative as you go around the course, coming up with different shots to match the situation at hand.

This is certainly true when it comes to the fade into the wind. While unconventional, this shot can be the perfect play from time to time. Learn how to hit this shot effectively, and learn how to turn over a draw as well, and you will be able to rise to the occasion when the wind comes up.

# CHAPTER 5: <u>LIE IN THE ROUGH</u>

The biggest problem with hitting a ball out of the rough is that you often don't know exactly what the problem is. Sometimes, the thick grass will grab the club and cause a shot to come up well short. Other times, the grass gets between the clubface and ball, causing a shot with no spin that flies and rolls farther than expected (the so-called "flyer.")

So how do you know what the ball will do when playing from the rough? There's always a little guesswork involved, but do your homework first and you'll eliminate much of the unknown. Any time you find the thick stuff, examine your ball with an eye on these clues:

**Ball sitting down:** If the rough is more than an inch tall, the ball will sometimes sink to the bottom. The grass will slow the club's speed and often cause the face to close through impact, sending the ball left.

**Ball sitting up:** If you've lucked into a fluffy lie, caution is still merited. For one, you may catch one of those flyer lies that send the ball into oblivion if you're not careful. Second, if it's perched really high, a lofted club may slip underneath the ball and hit it next to nowhere.

**The direction of the grass:** If the grain of the grass is growing against you, the ball won't travel as far. Hitting down-grain, expect the ball to "jump" and come out hot.

Whenever you're playing from tall rough, make a few practice swings near the ball to get a feel for the grass's thickness and resistance. Also, stand a little closer to the ball and focus on hitting down sharply. You want as little contact as possible with the grass, so a steeper swing is recommended.

## How to Read Your Lie in the Rough

Golf would be pretty easy if you could play every shot from the short grass. Of course, that is never going to be the case. Almost every golf course is lined with some kind of rough, and playing a shot from the rough is typically more difficult than playing the same shot from a fairway lie.

One of the skills that separate professional golfers from their amateur counterparts is the ability to hit quality shots from lies in the rough. By improving your ability to play from longer grass, you will be able to minimize the damage to your scorecard after one of your shots drifts offline.

In this chapter, we are going to address a specific part of playing from the rough – reading your lie. The way you prepare for a shot from the rough is almost as important as the swing itself. If you read your lie correctly and plan a smart shot as a result, you will be far more likely to enjoy a positive outcome.

Understanding how to read the lie of the ball in the rough isn't going to make these shots easy – but it can make them easier. You need to gain experience in order to read your rough lies properly, but the tips offered throughout the rest of this chapter will point you in the right direction.

A big part of learning how to read lies in the long grass comes down to understanding the course you are playing. Every course has rough which is uniquely based on the type of grass used, the length of the blades, the density of the grass, and more. Playing shots from the rough on one course may be relatively simple while playing the same kind of shot on another course could be nearly impossible.

When you stray from your home course to try out a new track, one of the first things you will want to do is get familiar with the rough. By understanding what you will face when your ball comes to rest in the rough, you can make the right adjustments to put your next shot back in position.

It is important to understand how to read your lie in the rough for both full swings and short game shots. The way you read your shots from the rough is going to depend entirely on the type of shot you need to play next, as chipping from the rough is totally different than hitting a seven iron, for instance. Only when you read the lie within the context of the shot you are facing will you be able to raise your level of play.

All of the content below is based on a right-handed golfer. If you happen to play left-handed, please take a moment to reverse the directions as necessary.

## The Inherent Challenge

The challenge of playing from the rough comes from the fact that you are going to lose control over the ball on these kinds of shots. When you play from the short grass, the club is able to cleanly contact the ball of the ball without any interference – assuming you do your job correctly.

With a clean strike, the grooves on your club are able to grab onto the ball, and backspin is created. That backspin both helps the ball get up in the air and help it hold its line as it flies. With sufficient backspin, you can control your shot and bring it to a stop in a timely manner when it lands.

All of that goes out the window, however, when playing from the rough. If you are in the long grass, there will be blades of grass trapped between the ball and the clubface at impact. What does that mean? Simple – your backspin rate is reduced, and the ball struggles to hold its line. Have you ever seen one of your shots 'zig-zag' in the air as it flew toward the target?

That was the result of a very low spin rate. Without the ability to impart backspin, you simply can't control the ball in the same way that you can when playing from the short grass. In the end, the ball goes in unpredictable directions, and it tends to bounce and roll a significant distance after it lands.

Golf is all about control, which is why it is so important to keep your ball out of the long grass whenever possible. You lose control when you venture into the rough, even if the rough on the course you are playing is not particularly deep. Rough doesn't have to be long in order to be penalizing – it simply has to be thick enough to cause contact problems between the clubface and the ball.

For full swing shots, the lack of backspin is a problem for a number of reasons. For one thing, you are going to have a hard time determining the distance of your shots. The ball will not fly as high as it does on a well-struck shot from the fairway, so you may experience distance loss.

However, the ball will sometimes come out 'quick' when played from a fluffy lie in the rough, opening up the possibility that your shot will travel too far. It is always going to be a bit of a guessing game from the rough, no matter how much experience you have on the links.

Another problem with full swings from the rough is getting the ball to stop. If you guess right on the carry distance, you may be able to land your shot on the green – but that doesn't mean it is going to stay there.

You don't have much backspin to work in your favor when it comes to stopping the ball, and the flat trajectory of your shot means it is likely to take a big bounce. Unless you are playing on a soft golf course, shots played from the rough will often need to be landed short of the target so they can run up toward the hole.

As you get closer to the green and transition into the short game, the picture doesn't get much better. From close range, you don't really have to worry about the trajectory issue, but the backspin reduction is still a problem.

Also, now that you are dealing with delicate shots, it can become hard to strike the ball cleanly enough to get it up into the air at all. A soft swing is likely to get caught up in the long grass, meaning your shot may travel just a matter of inches before coming to rest again. The ability to swing through the rough when chipping and pitching is a skill that all golfers should work hard to possess.

The difficulty of chipping from the rough largely comes down to the condition of the golf course you are playing. When on a soft course, you won't have much trouble – as long as you judge the lie pretty well, you should hit a decent shot. When conditions firm up, however, things get much more difficult.

Without enough backspin to stop your chips, you will need to use elevation to do the job, meaning you will have to hit high lobs and flop shots to stop the ball. These kinds of shots are never easy, and they carry a great degree of risk along with them. When playing a firm golf course, do everything you can to keep your ball on the short grass – playing from the rough is going to be a major challenge under such conditions.

## Reading Your Lie for Full Swing Shots

To get into some specifics on how you can read your lie in the rough, we are going to start with the topic of full swings. In the next section, we will discuss some of the points related to reading your lie for a chip or pitch shot around the green. For a clear understanding of what you should be looking for in the rough as you prepare to make a full swing, review the points listed below.

**Check the area immediately behind the ball.** The first thing you want to do as you walk up to your ball in the rough is to check out the area behind the ball (on the opposite side of the ball from the target). This is the side you will be hitting when you make your swing. Is there a lot of dense grass behind the ball, or only a few wispy strands?

Dense grass behind the ball is a bad sign, as many of those blades are going to be trapped between the clubface and the ball at impact. If the grass is thick in this area, your best option will likely be to punch out safely to the fairway.

However, if you catch a break and find only thin, light grass behind the ball, you may have a shot at the target.

**Check your swing path.** Moving back from the grass around the ball itself, you also need to check on your swing path as you approach impact. How does the grass look approximately a foot or so behind the ball? Is there any grass that may grab onto the club shaft and twist your club prior to contact?

This will usually not be the case, but it is an important point to check nonetheless. Again here, if you find that this is a trouble spot, choose to lay the ball up into the fairway with a wedge and eliminate the risk of going for a long shot from a bad lie.

**Is the ball sitting on the ground?** This is an important point, yet one that many golfers overlook. If the rough is rather dense, the ball may actually be sitting up in the air, as if on a tee. In other cases, where the blades of grass are weak, the ball will nestle all the way down to the bottom.

There are pros and cons to each of these situations. When the ball is sitting up, you will have an easier time accessing it at impact – however, you may make contact high on the face, causing the shot to come up short. If the ball is sitting down, it will be easier to make contact on the sweet spot – but you might have more difficulty getting to the ball in the first place. Always take note of how high the ball is sitting off the ground and keep that factor in mind as you plan your shot.

**Review your path to the target.** If you have strayed from the fairway and find your ball in the rough, there is a chance that you will have obstacles between yourself and the target – either in the air or on the ground. Obviously, it is trees that you will need to be most concerned about when in the air, while land-based obstacles can include water hazards, bunkers, and more.

Since shots from the rough tend to come out lower than shots from the fairway, you may need to pay closer attention to obstacles on the ground than you would otherwise. Once you have taken a good look at your path to the hole, you can decide whether you should go for the green or simply lay up for an easy approach.

It is important to know what to look for when stepping into the rough to play a shot. The points above should help point you in the right direction, but you are also going to need to gain experience before you can become comfortable with this part of the game.

Pay close attention to the result of each shot you hit from the rough, and think about how the lie of the ball may have affected the shot. Over time, you will become comfortable with how to read your lies, and your play will improve overall as a result.

## Reading Your Lie for Short Game Shots

Now that you are up around the green, you have different priorities when it comes to reading your lie. It is no longer as important to think about how easy it will be to get the ball up in the air since the ball only needs to travel a short distance before it lands anyway.

However, it is very important to think about control in this situation – specifically, you will be thinking about how well you can control the distance of the shot. As you read your short game lies in the rough, watch out for the following points.

**Air under the ball.** Just as was the case back when you were making a full swing, it is still important to think about how far the ball is off the ground when playing a chip or pitch. In fact, this point might be even more important when you are around the green.

If the ball happens to be sitting up a few inches off the ground, and you swing down toward the turf as you would do from the fairway, it is possible to miss the ball completely. Even if you do make contact, you will hit the ball high on the face and the shot will come up short. Carefully examine this part of your lie and adjust as necessary to make solid contact.

**Analyze thickness to pick the right club.** As you know, you can pick from a variety of different clubs when preparing to hit a chip shot. From a fairway lie, you could theoretically use any of the 14 clubs in your bag to knock the ball up onto the green, depending on the circumstances. That is not the case in the rough. Many of your clubs won't work to hit a good chip shot from a lie in the rough.

Generally speaking, you need to watch for the thickness of the grass when selecting a club. If the grass is rather thick, opt for your highest-lofted wedge, as it has a leading edge which will help to cut through the grass. If you find a slightly thinner lie, you may be able to go down to a gap wedge or even a pitching wedge to play the shot.

**Upslope or downslope.** In addition to the grass itself, the slope of the ground under your ball is going to have a lot to do with how you play this shot. If the ground is sloped up toward the target, you will naturally get more height on the shot – meaning you can bring the ball down softly without much trouble.

On the other hand, a chip out of the rough on a downslope is going to lead to a shot that comes out flat, takes a big bounce, and rolls out significantly. Playing from the rough on a downslope is one of the toughest spots you will find on the golf course.

**Any chance of spin?** Accurately predicting how much backspin you are going to put on the ball is your biggest challenge when chipping from any lie. Out of the rough, you will usually struggle to get any backspin at all – but that can change depending on your lie. If you have a decent lie in the rough, and the ball is sitting down on the turf, you might get a little spin.

Experience is going to play just as big of a role around the greens as it plays when hitting full shots. To accelerate your learning curve on this topic, try to find a local golf course that offers a practice chipping area. Drop some golf balls in the rough around the chipping green and read each lie before hitting your shot. If you make this a part of your regular practice routine, your skills in reading the rough are sure to improve quickly.

## Staying Out of the Rough

The one thing better than being able to accurately read your lie in the rough is being able to stay out of the rough in the first place. It will always be better to keep your ball on the short grass, so use the tips below to stay in play and away from the long grass as often as you can.

**Put away that driver.** Of course, it is fun to blast your driver as far as possible down the fairway, but doing so is not always going to be the smart play. Sometimes, you will be better off taking less club and playing for accuracy rather than power. When you are on the tee of a particularly narrow hole, put down the driver and choose something that you can safely put into the short grass.

**Take conservative lines with approach shots.** Rather than always firing directly at the flag, try aiming to the wide side of the green in an effort to stay away from the rough. This strategy will raise your percentage of greens hit in regulation, it will take some of the stress out of your game, and it will lower your scores.

**Use your curve to your advantage.** Nearly every golfer in the world has a fairly predictable shot pattern. You might not necessarily love your pattern, but you probably know what it is. Rather than trying to fight it, accept your shot shape for what it is at the moment, and use it to your advantage. By picking lines that will play to your strength, you can keep the ball in the short grass and out of trouble.

The best way to play good shots from the rough is to stay out of the rough. However, when you do venture into the long grass, use the advice contained above to read your lie accurately.

A combination of the advice in this chapter and plenty of experience should lead you to improvements on the course in the months and years ahead. Having confidence in your ability to play from the rough will help free you up on the rest of your shots, as you will know that you can get out of trouble if required.

◆ ◆ ◆

# CHAPTER 6: GREEN SPEED

C urious just how fast putts roll on your linoleum floor or synthetic putting green?

Want to know the speed of the surfaces on your home course? There's an app for that. It's called a Stimpmeter.

It's an ingeniously simple device – basically, a notched, V-shaped metal rail. The USGA sells its official Stimpmeter only to golf course superintendents or managers, so you'll have to obtain one through other means (such as an online auction site or retailer). You may also find instructions online for making your own Stimpmeter with materials found at any hardware store.

Some golf courses post their current green speeds on the Internet, in the pro shop, or near the practice green. However, most courses make this info readily available. You can always ask for it, but you'll likely get a ballpark figure that may or may not be accurate.

Before we explain how to measure green speed using a Stimpmeter, note that course management may take offense if they see you checking the pace of their greens. Some clubs like to flaunt their greens as "the fastest in town," while those whose surfaces lag behind aren't necessarily dying for potential customers to know. In other words, green speed can be a touchy subject.

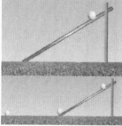

**Moving on... The Stimpmeter is easy to use. Just follow these steps:**

Find a flat portion of the surface being tested. It should be about 10' x 10'.

At the edge of the area, aim the bottom end of the device toward the area's center and place a ball in the notch; the Stimpmeter should lie flat on the ground.

Slowly lift the end closest to the notch until the ball is released. Hold the meter steady until the ball hits the surface.

Measure the distance between the ball's stopping point and the end of the Stimpmeter, then repeat the procedure twice more for accuracy.

The measurement, in feet and inches, is the Stimpmeter reading. For example, 10'6".

For comparison's sake, the greens on a typical public golf course "Stimp" at about 8 – 8.5". On the PGA Tour, greens are routinely 11' – 12', and sometimes 14' or higher for the Masters, U.S. Open, and a few other events.

## How to Measure Green Speed?

When you arrive at the golf course for a round, one of the first things you need to do is determine the speed of the greens for the day. Green speeds can change from day to day even on the same golf course – in fact, they can change from hole to hole as you go through the round.

There are a number of factors that come together to determine how fast or slow the greens will roll, and it is your job to pay attention to those factors in order to control your ball properly. It is safe to say that mastering the speed of the greens is one of your main jobs as a golfer, and it is one of the skills that will allow you to shoot low scores.

For professional golfers, figuring out green speeds is something that is always on the top of their to-do list. Touring pros play in a new location nearly every week, so they have to be able to adapt quickly in order to putt well. You probably don't travel to play golf quite like a Tour pro, but you are still likely to play a variety of courses throughout the year.

Developing the ability to gauge and then adjust to changing green speeds will make you a better player. Golf is a hard enough game as it is, but it becomes nearly impossible when you don't have a good feel for the speed of the putting surfaces.

In this chapter, we are going to look into the topic of measuring green speeds. There are really two ways you can view the question that is posed in the title of this chapter – you can think about literally measuring the green speeds, and you can think about 'measuring' in terms of learning how to control your ball on a given set of greens.

We are going to cover both of these topics. Actual measuring of green speeds is done with something called a Stimpmeter while learning how to putt on greens with a specific speed comes down to basic trial and error. When you are finished with this chapter, you should have a firm grasp on this topic from all angles.

It should be noted that green speeds affect more than just your putting during the course of a round. Sure, you need to have the speed of the greens down pat if you are going to putt well, but this topic also affects your chip shots, pitch shots, and even approach shots.

Any shot you hit with the goal of finding the green is going to be affected in some way by the speed of the greens. For this reason, the importance of reading the speed of the greens cannot be overstated. Take time before your round begins to focus on this point and you will be far more likely to succeed when the round gets started.

All of the content below is based on a right-handed golfer. If you happen to play left-handed, please take a moment to reverse the directions as necessary.

## Using a Stimpmeter

The Stimpmeter is a piece of golf maintenance equipment that was developed in 1935 by a man named Edward Stimpson. The device is extremely simple, and it has a very simple job to do. Basically, up until 1935, there was no way to accurately measure the speed of the greens on a golf course.

Players could say that greens were 'fast' or 'slow', but there was no objective way to put a number to those perceptions. That changed when Stimpson came up with his Stimpmeter. This device rolls the ball at a controlled speed each time it is used, so the distance of the rollout can be used to measure the speed of the greens in feet.

If you would like to measure the speed of the greens at your own club, you would simply need to acquire a Stimpmeter and then follow the directions below.

Bring the Stimpmeter and a few golf balls to the green that you would like to measure, along with a tee and a tape measure. You will need to find a flat section of the green on which to perform the test – measuring green speeds when going up or downhill is naturally going to skew the results. Not all greens have a flat section which is suitable for this test, so you may need to find just the right putting surface on the course before you can get an accurate reading.

With a flat section of the green located, you will need to mark a starting point for your test. One easy way to mark your starting point is by placing a tee into the putting surface. Place the ball into the notch in the Stimpmeter, and raise the device slowly until the ball falls out of the notch and rolls away. When the ball has come to a rest, measure the distance that it has traveled. This is your first reading.

Repeat this test two more times going in the same direction. When complete, move the Stimpmeter to the other side and run the test again, with the balls rolling in the opposite direction. Switching directions halfway through the test will allow you to negate the impact that the grain of the grass will have on green speeds. Once you have rolled the ball three more times from the other end, you will be done with the testing.

At this point, you should have six readings – three from each end of the flat section of green which was used for the test. To come to a final determination on green speed, add up these numbers and divide by six. This number, stated in feet, is the speed of the green according to the Stimpmeter.

You will often hear golfers refer to green speeds by just stating a single number, such as when somebody says the greens are 'running at a 10'. That means that the greens are running out an average of 10 feet when measured using the Stimpmeter. Fast greens will usually register readings up around 10 feet and beyond, with readings of 12 or more being common for professional tournaments.

Depending on the weather and other factors, the average golf course will usually come in around the 8-10' range. Anything slower than 8' or so is going to see like a pretty slow green by modern standards.

As a golfer, using a Stimpmeter can be a relatively interesting process, and it can show you have dramatically green speeds can vary from day to day (if you test regularly). However, as a practical tool to help you play better golf, the Stimpmeter doesn't really have much to offer.

Telling yourself that the greens are 'running at a 10' really isn't going to help you play better golf because that information is largely useless to your hands as you make a stroke. Instead of thinking about green speeds as a number, you should be more concerned with how the greens 'feel' when you are putting or chipping. In the next section, we will discuss how you can measure green speeds in a practical way which will lead to improved performance on the course.

## Practical Measurement of Green Speeds

For most golfers, there is no need to purchase a Stimpmeter. You can leave that piece of equipment to the maintenance staff at your golf course, as it isn't going to do much for your performance. Instead, the best way to 'measure' green speeds before you play is simply to arrive early and spend some time on the practice green.

Warmup putting is not only about getting your stroke in order for the day – it is also about learning the speed of the greens. In fact, it could easily be argued that the single most important thing you need to do before teeing off is to learn the green speeds. Without this piece of information in your mist as you walk to the first tee, you will almost certainly struggle over the first few holes until you make the necessary adjustments.

While most golfers do manage to make their way to the practice green before they tee off, most waste this time by just hitting a few putts without any rhyme or reason. If you are actually going to dial in your speed control before you tee off, you need to have a plan for your warm-up putting session. Consider using the process below to get yourself ready to play (of course, this process can be tweaked as necessary to suit your needs and preferences).

To start, take your putter and three golf balls from the bag. Find a long stretch of open green and hit some long putts from one side of the green to the other. It is typical for most golfers to start out with short putts, but you will get far more benefit from rolling long putts at this point. Use the edge of the green on the other side as a target for your putts – try to roll the ball up as close to the edge as possible without going off the green.

As you roll these long putts, pay close attention to the speed of the practice green. Are your putts rolling out farther than you expect, or do they seem to be stopping quickly? It should actually only take a few long putts for you to start to get an idea for the green speeds on the day.

With your long putting completed, find somewhere on the green where you can hit a 15-footer to a hole. Place all three golf balls down on the ground and hit each toward the hole you picked out 15' away. The goal with these putts is to get them at least to the hole, but don't allow them to roll more than a couple of feet past.

At this point, you are really testing your ability to control your ball on the green. If you are coming up short with your 15-footers, you will know the greens are slightly slower than you expect. Or, on the other hand, if the ball is running out several feet past the cup, the greens are fast and you need to adjust your stroke accordingly. Repeat this three-ball drill until you feel comfortable with your speed control from mid-range.

Finally, it is time to hit some short putts. Drop your golf balls at around 3'-4' from the cup and knock them in one at a time. Short putts don't change much based on the speed of the greens, but you do need to be careful not to be too aggressive when the greens are fast. After you have holed several short putts consecutively, you will be ready for the first tee.

As you can see, you don't need to hit a large number of putts in order to prepare yourself for the green speeds you are going to see on the course. The entire process listed above shouldn't take more than 15 minutes or so, and that time will be well spent when you get out onto the course and already have a great feel for the putting surfaces. While your playing partners are spending the first few holes trying to get dialed in, you will be ready to make putts starting on the very first green.

## Adjusting on the Course

The preparation that you do prior to hitting the first tee is going to go a long way toward helping you putt at a high level. Unfortunately, that preparation is not always perfect, however, as some courses will have greens that vary in speed between the practice area and the actual course. If you get out onto the course to find that the greens are a different speed than what you expected, it will be important to adjust as quickly as possible.

No matter how much preparation you have done on the practice green, you should always be paying close attention to the first few putts that you hit during your round. Putts coming up well short or rolling out well past the hole are obviously cause for concern, as those are sure signs that the green speeds on the course are not going to match up with the practice green. Take note of any big differences that you find between the practice green and the course and adjust right away.

While you can't necessarily predict which way this adjustment will go, it is more common for the practice green to be faster than the course, rather than the other way around. With so much foot traffic on the practice green each day, it will often become firm and fast – at least, firmer and faster than the greens on the golf course. This is not a hard and fast rule, of course, but don't be surprised to find greens on the course that run a bit slower than what you expected.

Another thing you need to consider while on the course is the geography of the land around each green. For instance, a green that is sitting down in a bowl will usually have more water available to it, meaning the grass will be lusher and the surface will be slower overall. On the other hand, a green that is sitting up on a perch will usually be fast due to a lack of water and the drying effects of the wind. Experienced golfers look at not only the green itself to get a read but also at the surrounding terrain.

Speaking of the surrounding terrain, check for trees around the green which may be blocking sunlight from reaching the putting surface. An abundance of trees will prevent the sun from drying up the green, meaning your putts will likely run slower than they will on greens which get plenty of sun.

While you don't want to overwhelm yourself with details as you try to predict green speeds, it is important to take all relevant information into consideration before you hit the putt.

It is important to note that the job of adjusting to green speeds is never complete. You can never really get comfortable on this point, as things can change throughout the day that will impact how quickly your ball runs across the green. Always pay close attention to how your ball behaves and be willing to adapt quickly in order to achieve the best possible results with your flat stick.

## In-Round Changes to Green Speeds

As was just mentioned above, you can't count on greens remaining the same speed from the start of a round on through to the finish. After all, rounds of golf regularly take more than four hours to complete, which is plenty of time for the condition of the greens to change significantly. What kind of events can occur which will impact the speed of the greens? Check out the list below for a better understanding of this topic.

**Bright sunshine.** You don't need to be a professional landscaper to know that grass is going to grow quickly under bright sunshine. When the sun comes out in the afternoon, you can expect the blades of grass on the greens to grow quickly until sunset. Of course, that means your putts are going to get slower and slower as the day wears on.

If you look carefully, you might even be able to see your footprints on the greens as you step on the freshly-grown surface. Take note of this possibility and hit your putts a bit harder as the afternoon turns into evening.

**Rain.** A rainy day is pretty much the opposite of a sunny day, yet both of these weather conditions will have the same effect on the greens. When the rain comes down during your round, you can again expect the surfaces to get slower. Water will sit on top of the green for a short amount of time after it falls, offering resistance to your putts.

Not only should you hit your putts harder on wet greens, but you should also play slightly less break as well. Hitting your putts harder will cause the ball to hold its line long after it is struck, meaning you don't need to give the ball quite as much room to turn into the hole.

**Strong winds.** Unlike the first two points on our list, the wind is one weather condition that will actually serve to speed up the greens. If a strong wind kicks up during your round, moisture is going to be pulled out of the putting surfaces – and your putts will become faster as a result.

When taking this factor into account, be sure that the green in question is actually affected by the wind. Greens that are protected by another terrain will not be dried out as quickly as greens that are exposed to the elements.

**Dew evaporation.** When you start your round early in the day, you may encounter some dew on the first few holes. This dew is not a big deal, although it will cause the greens to be a bit slower than they would be otherwise. Of course, that means the greens are going to speed up as the day goes on and the dew evaporates away. As you see the dew gets lighter and lighter, plan on the greens playing faster as a result.

It is nearly impossible to play good golf without having control over the speed of the greens. This is a topic that seems relatively simple, yet it can get quite complicated as you learn more and more about what goes into the speed of putting surfaces.

To give yourself the best chance to putt well during a given round, be sure to arrive early to spend some time on the practice green. Once on the course, pay close attention to how your putts are rolling out and adjust your stroke accordingly.

◆ ◆ ◆

# CHAPTER 7: <u>HOW TO READ THE WIND</u>

P rofessional golfers can get downright obsessive about the wind. Of course, when the slightest gust can make a quarter-million-dollar difference in your paycheck, that's understandable.

Wind tends to affect the better golfer more than a novice or high-handicapper because skilled players hit higher shots that spend more time in the air. Unless you hit one ground ball after another, though, you should pay at least a little attention to what the wind is doing.

The most common trick is to toss a small handful of grass into the air to confirm the wind's direction and force. However, this only tells you what's happening where you're standing. What's the wind doing between you and the target?

If you're playing an approach to the green, look at the flag. If it's still or barely moving, it may be blocked by surrounding trees – look at their tops for additional clues. Keep an eye out for nearby flagpoles, even give the clouds a brief glance to determine the wind's general pattern.

Here's another tip that will help you throughout a round: Note the direction of the wind at the clubhouse or the first hole, then open your scorecard to the graphic course layout depiction (included on most cards). Lightly draw an arrow on the layout to match the wind's direction, then refer to the card any time you're uncertain.

A final note: Unless you're a pro or an amateur with a single-digit handicap, don't spend more than a few seconds gauging the breeze. You'll only slow-down play, and likely draw a few eye rolls from your playing partners.

## How to Read and Adjust to the Wind

The wind is one of the most difficult variables you will have to deal with on the golf course. In fact, it can easily be said that playing on a windy day is one of the toughest challenges in all of golf. A course that would normally be rather mundane and simple can be made into quite the test simply through the presence of some wind.

While it is well known that playing into the #wind will cost you yardage, golfers often underestimate the impact of the wind when it is blowing in other directions. No matter where the wind is coming from, it needs to be respected for its ability to impact your shots.

In this chapter, we are going to take a close look at how $wind influences your play on the golf course. We will talk about how you can do a good job of reading the %wind, and how you can adjust for the wind to give your shots the best possible chance at success.

Nothing we can say in this chapter will suddenly make it easy to play on a windy day – this is always going to be a challenge – but we hope to at least give you a fighting chance at a good score.

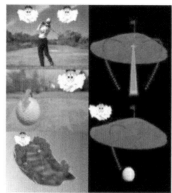

Of course, the frequency with which you have to play in the wind is going to depend on where you live and where you play your golf. Some regions of the world are simply more prone to wind than others.

Also, even within small regions, some golf courses are located in spots where the wind is more likely to blow. Courses that are set along a coastline, for example, often require golfers to deal with a steady breeze – if not a powerful wind. With that said, it is important for all golfers to know how to play in the wind, even if it is not a challenge that you encounter on a regular basis.

If you play this game long enough, you are sure to end up on the course on a windy day from time to time. Or, you may take a trip to play golf in an area where the wind is more common. Whatever the case, you should have a wind strategy in mind that you can use as soon as the breeze picks up.

It would be a shame to have to give up on your scoring goals for the day just because you aren't comfortable playing in the wind. Yes, this will always be a tough task, but the challenge of this game is a big part of what makes it so fun.

If golf were easy, you would probably only play for a short period of time before picking up a new hobby. Golf is difficult – just embrace that fact, and do the best you can. You are going to be tested when playing in the wind, so get ready for the battle and expect to come out on top.

All of the content below is based on a right-handed golfer. If you happen to play left-handed, please take a moment to reverse the directions as necessary.

# Playing in the Wind – The Basics

Before we get into some more detailed instructions later in the chapter, we wanted to start with an outline of some basic @wind tips. If you don't have any idea of how you should go about playing golf on a windy day, this section is the perfect place to start. None of the tips listed below is groundbreaking in any way, but they will help point you in the right direction.

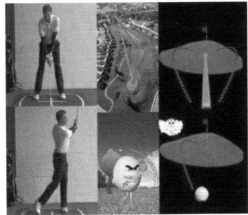

**Swing softer.** This is the first thing you should do when the #wind starts to pick up. Unfortunately, most amateur golfers take the opposite approach. When the wind starts to blow, the average player will swing harder and harder, trying to overpower the breeze.

You are never going to be able to overpower Mother Nature. The $wind is always stronger than you, so don't bother trying to swing extra hard and force the ball to the target. Instead, make controlled swings and use strategy to your advantage. When you make soft swings, your backspin rate will be reduced and the ball will stay lower to the ground.

This is a good thing. Hitting the ball high is going to allow the wind to have a powerful effect over your shots, which is not the result you should desire. Swing soft, keep the ball down, and maintain as much control over your ball flights as possible.

**Use a conservative game plan.** You simply can't expect to be as accurate with your shots on a windy day as you would be when the conditions are calm. The presence of wind is going to widen the dispersion of your shots, so you should pick targets that allow for some forgiveness.

Imagine this example – you are hitting your second shot into a par four, and you have 150 yards to the hole. The hole is located near the right edge of the green, close to a water hazard. Normally, on a calm day, you would have the confidence to aim close to this flag, since you only have 150 yards to go.

On a breezy day, however, you should take more caution. Aim away from the water, toward the middle of the green, and give yourself some margin for error. Even if that means you don't hit the ball quite as close to set up a birdie putt, at least you should stay out of the pond and avoid a penalty stroke. You can use this kind of thinking all the way around the course when playing in the wind. Be smart, play conservative, and do your best to keep your ball in play.

**Be patient.** Some frustrating things are going to happen to you over the course of a full round which is played on a windy day. You will probably hit at least a couple of shots that feel great coming off the club and look great in the air – until the %wind blows them in the wrong direction.

It will be easy to lose your patience along the way, as you will feel like you aren't being rewarded for your efforts. Do your best to keep your temper under control and stay patient all the way through the last green. Sure, golf in the wind can seem unfair, but the wind is outside of your control. You can control your effort and your attitude, so spend your energy on those points and let the rest of it go.

**Lower your expectations.** If you are the kind of golfer who likes to set scoring goals for each round before you head to the first tee, it would be wise to lower your expectations slightly based on the conditions. As mentioned above, there is nothing you can do about the conditions on the course. They are going to make the day more challenging, and you should alter your scoring expectations slightly.

This doesn't mean you should give up on the idea of playing a good round – you just don't want to set the bar so high that you wind up frustrated early on. Even if you do like to set daily scoring goals, consider skipping that step on a windy day, and just commit yourself to do your best. You might find it easier to maintain a patient attitude if you aren't constantly thinking about reaching an arbitrary scoring target.

As you gain experience playing in the wind, some of the points listed above will begin to come naturally. You will automatically know not to expect as much when playing in the wind, and you will pick safer targets by default. Until you reach that level of experience, however, keep these points near the front of your mind and use them to guide your play on a difficult windy day.

## Reading the Wind Accurately

To make an obvious point, you can't see the @wind. Sure, you can see the results of the #wind – flags pointing in a specific direction, tree branches swaying, etc. – but you can't actually see the air being blown from one place to another.

This inherently makes reading the wind more difficult than reading a putt, for example. When reading your putts, you can see the slope of the ground and adjust your line accordingly. Reading the wind will never be that easy, although there are some steps you can take to make it a bit easier.

To start with, all golfers should know how to read $wind with the help of a few blades of grass. Even if you haven't used this method for yourself, you've likely seen the professional golfers use it on TV.

On a windy day, many pro golfers will choose to reach down to grab a few blades of grass that they can toss up into the air in order to judge the %wind. When you toss the grass up, it will quickly be blown in the same direction as the wind. This is an accurate and efficient way to get a good understanding of wind direction.

Unfortunately, you can't really stop there. Tossing grass up into the air will give you a good understanding of the wind where you are standing, but the ball is going to be flying high up into the air as it heads toward the target – what is the wind doing up there? That information is more valuable for your purposes. If you are playing on a tree-lined golf course, you can look to the tops of the trees for help.

They may be moving in the same direction as the grass you just tested, or they could be doing something completely different. Only when you gather up as much information as possible will you be able to make a smart decision on the true impact the wind will have on your shot.

If there are no trees around, you will need to hope to find something else that is up in the air which can guide your understanding of the wind. You may be able to find a flag on top of a building somewhere in the distance, or perhaps some smoke coming out of a chimney. Whatever the case, look around for any help you can get and then add that information to your calculations prior to hitting the shot.

As a final option, you can just use your own personal feel for the day as a way to gauge the wind. What direction does the wind feel like it is coming from overall? Sometimes, when in the middle of the course, you can get tricked by little swirls of wind that will make it seem like the wind is suddenly blowing from a new direction.

Rarely will that actually be true? The prevailing wind direction is likely to hold throughout your round, so figure it out early on and then trust it for the rest of the day.

# CHAPTER 8: <u>RECOVER FROM THE TREES</u>

M ost golfers have a deathly fear of water hazards and sand traps ..but a ball in the trees can present even bigger problems.

There are a number of ways to escape the woods depending on where your ball sits. Even with a clear swing and a path through the trees, discretion is the better part of valor. It's usually best to take your medicine and use the least risky path back to safety

When tree-bound, always note overhanging branches between your golf ball and the target. Use a long-iron, mid-iron, or even a hybrid to ensure a low enough shot to escape, play the ball slightly back in your stance, and swing with a firm wrist to keep the golf ball down. On the other hand, going over limbs may be a better choice if you have a decent lie.

If you've gotten unlucky and find your ball beneath low-hanging limbs, assess your options. If the ball simply can't be hit, take an unplayable lie following USGA rules.

If you can advance the ball, make sure you're able to take a stance and swing without bending or breaking limbs or leaves. Removing obstacles from your swing path – as in breaking a branch on the backswing – carries a one-shot penalty.

If you play at least some of your golf on a tree-lined course, you are going to find yourself in the middle of those trees from time to time.

Despite your best efforts to keep the ball in the fairway, a drive or two is sure to get away from you on occasion. When you do lose your way and wind up in the woods, you need to have a plan to get back on track as soon as possible.

Hitting your ball into the trees has the potential to cost you several strokes on the scorecard, but it doesn't have to end that way. Make smart decisions, execute your recovery shot, and keep the damage to a minimum.

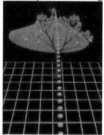

In this chapter, we are going to offer some advice on how to get out of this situation successfully. There are a number of variables at play anytime you find your ball in the trees since no two situations are exactly alike.

The golfer who fares the best in these spots will be the one who is willing to be creative and patient at the same time. You can't just close your eyes and swing hard in order to get out of this kind of trouble. You'll need a smart plan, and we hope that the information offered in this chapter will help improve your ability to craft such a plan.

All of the content below is written from the perspective of a right-handed golfer. If you happen to play left-handed, please take a moment to reverse the directions as necessary.

## The Basics

There are a few basic concepts that you should have in mind when you hit the ball in the trees. In this section, we are going to highlight these points, and they should serve as the groundwork for your thinking when you head into the woods to play a recovery shot.

You'll always want to have an open mind, of course, as you never know exactly what you will face in this type of situation. However, as long as you keep these concepts in the back of your mind, you should be on the way toward a successful conclusion.

**Calm down.** The first rule of thumb to follow when your ball is in the trees is to calm down and think through the situation rationally. When you first see your ball head into the woods, you are going to be frustrated – or even angry. Obviously, you weren't intending on hitting your ball into the trees, so you've made some sort of mistake to wind up in this predicament.

Many mistakes made in the trees stem from the fact that the player has not yet calmed down and focused on the task at hand. It is natural to get frustrated when playing a game as difficult as golf, but you've got to get your mind back on track as soon as possible.

Before you arrive at your ball, work through the frustration of the poor shot, and put it behind you. With your temper set to the side, you can focus on nothing other than playing the best possible shot given the situation at hand.

**The top priority is getting out.** Everyone loves the thought of playing a brilliant shot from deep in the woods. You may have visions of the ball zooming out of the trees, missing all the branches, and landing softly on the putting surface. Is this possible? Maybe – depending on a number of factors, including your lie, the path you have to the hole, the length of the shot, and more.

However, no matter how badly you want to pull off an incredible shot, your first task is simply to get the ball back on the short grass. That might mean going for the green, or it might mean just pitching out to the fairway. When in doubt, opt for the safer shot so you don't put yourself in even deeper trouble. Playing it safe and pitching out might not be the most exciting option in the world, but it is often the best bet.

**Need more than a 'window'.** Many golfers get themselves into trouble by aiming at a small 'window' of an opening in the trees that wait between their ball and the green. While it might be technically possible to squeeze the ball through that opening, is it likely?

Not so much. It is tremendously difficult to hit a small opening in the trees with a golf shot, as there are countless things that could go wrong along the way. Judging both the height and direction of your shot is a serious challenge under the best of circumstances, and that doesn't even take into account the pressure of pulling it off when even a slight miss will lead to an ugly result. You should be looking for large openings when plotting your path out of the trees.

**Take the conditions into consideration.** If you are playing on a dry and firm golf course, playing the ball out of the trees using a low path is probably going to be your best bet. With any luck, you'll be able to get the ball down on the fairway and let it run up toward the green. Of course, when the course is wet and soft, that really isn't going to work.

The fairway won't offer much run-out, meaning your punch out isn't going to make much progress. You can still take the low path if it is your best bet, but you shouldn't expect to see as much run out that you would see when the course is dry.

The high option is far more desirable in soft conditions, assuming it is available. This way, you can cover maximum distance through the air, and you can trust the ball to stop quickly when it lands (giving you a bit more control over the shot).

**Develop your own style.** While you should always err on the safe side when trying to get out of the trees, you should also feel welcome to develop your own style on these shots. For instance, some players love to hit low punch shots through the trees and back to the fairway.

Other players will look high whenever possible, preferring to loft the ball over the branches and back to the short grass. Also, some golfers are naturally more conservative than others. You might find that you prefer to just pitch out in nearly every circumstance, or you may find that you are comfortable going for the green with the circumstances line up just right.

Patience is an important word when you find your ball resting amongst the trees. It is easy to get annoyed at yourself for finding this situation in the first place, and that frustration can lead you to some poor decisions. Take a deep breath or two, calm yourself down, and be patient with your plan. You might not like playing the safe shot but doing so will probably be in the best interest of your overall score.

## Learning Some Valuable Shots

Making good decisions is a big part of successfully getting out of the trees in a single swing. However, you can't succeed in decision making alone. Once you decide how you are going to attempt to get back to the short grass, you still have to execute the shot. If you fail to execute, all the brilliant planning in the world isn't going to be worth anything in the end.

In this section, we are going to highlight three valuable shots you can use to move your ball out of the woods and back to the fairway – or even up to the green. It is easy enough to practice these shots on the range, even though you won't be playing from the trees in that setting. Learn how to manipulate the flight of the ball in practice and you'll have more options available to you when on the course.

The points below highlight the three main kinds of shots you'll want to have available when you have to play out of the trees.

**A low punch.** This is where it all starts. Many of the shots you play to get out of the trees will need to be hit low in order to avoid branches. This type of shot will fly very low – maybe even just a few feet off the ground – before landing and running the rest of its distance.

To play a low punch, you will need to make a couple of key adjustments.

First, you will choke down significantly on the grip at address, in order to shorten the length of the swing. Then, you are going to move the ball well back in your stance. Roughly halfway between your right foot and the center point of your stance is a good rule of thumb.

When you combine these two adjustments with a low-lofted club – something like a three iron or four iron – you will be set up for a beautiful low punch. As far as the swing itself is concerned, your job is simple. You are going to stay balanced, make a short backswing, and hit down through the ball with confidence. A clean strike is crucial here, so make that your main objective.

**A high escape.** On the other end of the spectrum, you may need to use a high shot from time to time to get out of the woods. The kind of high shot you will want to hit from the trees is somewhat different from the kinds of high shots you may hit from the fairway.

Thanks to the high spin rates offered by modern golf balls, it is possible to hit shots that start low and gradually climb until they wind up quite high in the air. Those shots are excellent from the fairway but are usually not very useful from the trees. If you need to get over some trees, you will want to hit a shot that launches high right from the start.

To achieve this goal, move the ball up in your stance and open the face of your club slightly. Then, as you make the swing, be sure to stay back with your body so you can swing through impact on a level plane. It takes skill to execute this kind of shot, but it's not impossible.

**A dramatic curve.** In some cases, you may need to hit a sharp hook in order to get out of the trees while keeping the ball on the right path. In other cases, it will be a big fade/slice. Being able to snap the ball in either direction is a great advantage when you are trying to get out of the trees while still moving the ball up toward the green.

If you would like to attempt some major hooks and slices, start by making a change to your stance. As a good rule of thumb, you are going to point the clubface in the direction that you would like the ball to end up, and you are going to set your feet in the direction that you want the ball to start.

As an example, for a shot that you want to hook out of the trees and up to the green, you would aim the clubface at the green and set your feet on a line that takes you away from the trees and out toward the fairway.

Then, you swing along the line set up by your feet, and hopefully, a hook is the result. This is a risky shot, of course, because if the ball happens to fly straight instead of hooking as desired, you will end up way off course.

You are going to struggle to get out of the trees successfully if you don't have at least a couple of the shots listed above at your disposal. Making your standard swing just isn't going to work in all situations, and that is particularly true when you are in the middle of the woods.

Take some time to practice these shot variations during an upcoming range session and you'll be better prepared for the next time you find the trees off the tee.

◆ ◆ ◆

# CHAPTER 9: OVER THE TOP

**M**any golfers suffer from a swing that approaches the ball in an "over-the-top" fashion, causing a variety of mishits such as slices and pulled shots.

An over-the-top golf swing path typically results when the golfer's arms start the downswing – big mistake. Instead, the lower body should lead the way, pulling the shoulders, arms, and club toward the ball from an inside path.

There are a number of drills to promote proper body rotation and cure the over-the-top syndrome. One of the best may just be the simplest.

**Here's how it's done:**

1.Using any club, assume your normal address position and begin the backswing.

2. On reaching the top of the swing, pause for a full two seconds.

3. Finish the swing.

Pausing prevents the arms and hands from taking over on the transition from backswing to downswing. You should feel the left side of your lower body (for right-handers) begin to turn toward the target before the hands start downward.

Golfers looking for a quick fix for an over-the-top swing can try another trick: At address, move your left foot about six inches forward so that your stance is closed in relation to the target line. Keep the clubface aimed at the target and swing normally.

## Stop Coming Over the Top in Your Golf Swing

Three of the most dreaded words in the game of golf are 'over the top'. A swing that includes an over the top move during the transition from the backswing to the downswing is one that will always be prone to hitting a slice.

As you certainly are aware, the slice is among the biggest issues that stand between amateur golfers and shooting better scores. If you are a player that struggles with the slice, removing the over the top mistake from your swing has the potential to change your game almost overnight.

Obviously, eliminating your over the top move is going to be easier said than done. It is an easy mistake to make, and if you have been swinging the club in this manner for a long time, your old habits aren't going to go away without a fight.

To correct your swing technique, you will first need to understand what you are doing wrong to create the over the top move in the first place. After you understand the root cause of the problem, you can then get down to work on fixing it.

A slice is not the only negative outcome that you can experience when swinging the club over the top. Other problems you can face include the following –

**Too much backspin.** An over the top swing will approach the ball from a steep angle, meaning that you may impart too much backspin onto your shots. While that isn't necessarily a big deal when hitting your short irons, it can be a big problem with your driver.

**Loss of distance.** This issue is directly related to putting too much backspin on your shots. A high spin rate will send the ball floating up into the air, costing you valuable distance. To add yardage to your shots you will have to find a way to get rid of your over the top move in order to reduce the backspin rate effectively.

**One dimensional game.** It is almost impossible to hit a draw when making an over the top swing. That means that all of your shots are going to fall into the fade or slice category, making you a one dimensional player out on the course. Even if you prefer to play a fade most of the time, it is helpful to have the ability to hit an occasional draw when necessary.

There is nothing good that comes from swinging the club over the top. While you might be able to find a way to play decent golf using this kind of motion, your game will be better for the effort if you can put in the practice time to get rid of it once and for all. This is not an impossible task, but it will require some focused practice and plenty of patience.

All of the instruction contained below is based on a right-handed golfer. If you play left-handed, please reverse the directions as needed.

## A Clear Picture of the Problem

Do you know exactly what it means to come 'over the top' in your golf swing? Most players think that they are familiar with this swing problem, but it might be a little more complicated than you realize. Only when you fully understand the over the top swing fault, and its root cause, can you get down to work on taking it out of your game.

Over the top refers to the motion of your swing during the transition from backswing to downswing. Instead of your hands (and the club) moving down toward the ground as you transition forward, your hands move up and away from your body in an over the top swing.

The result is a swing plane that is too high coming down into the ball, leading to a steep angle of attack that swipes across the ball from outside to in. Both the steep angle of attack and the outside-in swing path are negative elements that can lead to poor ball striking. Simply put, a player who is struggling with an over the top swing needs to reverse the pattern of movement they are using during the transition.

Instead of the club moving up and away from the body, it needs to move down and in closer to the body. This might feel awkward to someone who is used to swinging with an over the top move, but it is a necessary change if better ball striking is going to be achieved.

While the over the top action itself happens at the top of the swing, signs of trouble can usually be seen much earlier than that. In fact, most golfers who swing the club over the top make a killer mistake during the takeaway portion of the swing. After this mistake is made during the takeaway, an over the top swing is all but inevitable. So what is that mistake? Taking the club too far to the inside.

Ideally, the club will swing straight back from the ball early in the takeaway. The first few inches of the takeaway are crucial to set up the path for the rest of the swing. If you are able to keep the clubhead on a straight back path away from the ball early in the swing, you will be in a good position. However, if you allow the club to swing inside early, you will be setting yourself up for an over the top move.

Most of the time, the inside takeaway can be blamed on overactive hands. A good takeaway is made by using the rotation of the shoulders and torso to move the club – but many amateur golfers make the mistake of using their hands instead. By using your hands to move the club away from the ball, you will put the club on an inside path and an over the top motion is the likely result.

Why does an inside takeaway lead to an over the top swing? It all comes down to space. You need to have space available to swing your hands down toward impact in the forward swing. When you make an inside takeaway, you are bringing your hands and the club in very close to your body.

As you finish the backswing, you will likely find that there is no space available to then swing down into the shot. The only option is to take the club over the top, simply to create space and give your hands a free and clear path to the ball. While this move will allow you to make contact with the ball, it won't enable you to hit the kind of quality shots that you would like to see come off your clubs.

The answer to this problem, of course, is to make a wider backswing. When you are able to maintain width between your hands and your body in the backswing, there will be plenty of room to swing down toward impact.

You won't have to take the club over the top because you will have a clear path from the top of your backswing directly to the ball. Using a takeaway that keeps your hands quiet and allows the shoulders to do the work is the best way to create a wide swing and eliminate the over the top error.

## Two Great Drills

It is helpful to understand the problem of making an over the top move in your swing – but understanding alone isn't enough to successfully fix it. For that, you will want to use a couple of drills that have been specifically designed to address this problem. If you can spend some practice time working on each of the two drills highlighted below, you should be able to solve your over the top problem and get your golf swing back on track.

The first drill will address your takeaway since that is where the trouble starts for most players. Your takeaway is a part of the swing that probably hasn't received a lot of attention over the years.

Most golfers work on things like swing plane and impact position while overlooking the importance of the takeaway. This drill isn't going to be the most exciting thing you have ever done at a golf course, but it will be one of the best things you have done to improve your game.

**To complete the takeaway drill, follow the steps below –**

To start, take out one of your mid-irons (such as a seven iron) and take your stance as if you were going to hit a shot. You won't be hitting any actual shots during this drill, so there is no need to have any golf balls in front of you. Place a club on the ground instead of a golf ball, and position that club so that the shaft is representing your (imaginary) target line for the shot.

Once you are into your stance, drop your right hand off of the club and place it in your right pocket (or on your hip if you don't have pockets). At this point, your left hand will be the only thing holding onto the club.

Start your swing and take the club back until it is parallel with the ground using only your left hand. You should quickly find that you need to engage your shoulders to make a smooth takeaway since you only have one of your two hands available to control the club. When you reach a position where the club is parallel to the ground, stop your swing and pause.

Check the angle of the shaft of your club at this point. If you have made a good takeaway, the club will be parallel to the club that is on the ground representing your target line. Reaching this position successfully is a good sign of a proper takeaway. However, if the angle of the shaft is pointing behind you, you will know you have moved the club too far to the inside. Repeat the drill over and over until you can avoid the inside takeaway.

The idea of this drill is to take your hands out of the takeaway and force you to rely on your shoulders and torso to move the club. It will be harder to take the club on an inside path when only your left hand is holding onto the grip. After several repetitions of this drill, put your right hand back on the club and make a few practice swings. Remember what you learned and focus on avoiding the inside takeaway even when you have both hands on the club.

The other drill that will help you eliminate your over the top move is called the 'towel swing'. This is another drill where you won't even hit the golf ball – however, don't let that cause you to think that the drill is not important. The lessons that you can learn from completing the towel swing drill will quickly translate to your normal swing when you start hitting some balls on the range.

**Use the steps below to properly complete the towel drill –**

For this drill, you will need a large golf towel (or a towel from home that you don't mind using for this purpose). Lay the towel out on the ground and roll it up along the longest side. When you are finished rolling it up, you should be left with a long cylinder shape.

In one end of the rolled-up towel, tie a knot that will be used to keep the towel from unrolling. You might find that it is easier to tie this knot if you roll the towel up tightly in the previous step.

Once your knot is in place, pick up the towel by the non-knotted end. You are going to now pretend that this towel is your golf club, and the end with the knot will act as the clubhead. Take your regular golf grip around the rolled-up towel and take your stance as normal.

With your stance in place, try to make a golf swing using the towel. In order to do this successfully, you are going to need to make a smooth, slow swing with great tempo. If you try to rush the swing, the towel will not come along for the ride.

The transition is the trickiest part of this drill. Should you try to move your hands over the top, the towel won't cooperate (and may even hit you in the back). However, if you make a wide backswing and drop your hands down perfectly during the transition, you should find that you are able to swing through the hitting area nicely.

After plenty of repetitions swinging the towel, pick up a golf club, and hit a few short shots. Think about how your swing felt while using the towel and try to replicate that feeling with your clubs. When done correctly, this quick and simple drill can actually take the over the top move out of your swing.

## Adapting to Your New Swing

With enough practice time spent on the two drills above, you should be able to take the over the top flaw out of your swing. What you will be left with is a more powerful, more consistent swing that you can rely on throughout a round. However, that doesn't mean that you will instantly shoot better scores. Since you are used to playing with an over the top swing, you might find that you have trouble translating your better mechanics into lower numbers.

The biggest problem is aim. As an over-the-top player, you have learned how to aim your shots in such a way that will allow you to get away with the poor ball flights you were generating. Now that your ball flight is better, you have to correct the way you aim your shots.

Most likely, you have gotten used to aiming a little bit left of the target so that you can fade or slice the ball back online. Now, with your slice gone, you will need to aim closer to the actual target itself. Focus on your aim on the driving range so you can build trust in this idea before you test it on the course.

The other adjustment you will need to make is to the distance that you expect from each of your clubs. If you are attacking the ball from a flatter angle, it is almost certain that you will have gained distance over your previous swing. Your short irons may fly around the same yardage as they did before, but expect your long irons and woods to have dramatically increased.

Pay attention to how far your shots are flying with your new swing and adapt as quickly as possible. Your scores are only going to start to come down when you are able to pull the right club for the distance at hand on a regular basis.

With less backspin being imparted on your golf ball at impact, you can plan on a lower overall flight as part of your new trajectory. That means that wind will be less of a factor. You still need to account for wind when preparing to hit a shot, but it likely won't have the same effect that it did when you were coming over the top. Since wind is hard to predict and difficult to account for properly, limiting the effect that it has on your shots is always a good thing.

# Trust Your Preparation

No matter how hard you work on the driving range, there will always be a point on the course where you doubt yourself and are tempted to go back to your old swing. Don't fall for this temptation.

You worked on making swing changes for a reason, and you will become a better player in the long run now that you have eliminated your over the top move. Even if the results aren't great during your first round or two on the course, stay with the plan and trust that you will continue to get better.

Your trust in this new swing will grow with experience, both from hitting balls on the driving range and from playing rounds on the course. Hit practice balls regularly to engrain the new fundamentals of your swing, and try to play a couple of rounds on your own as well.

Playing golf by yourself will give you a chance to get comfortable with your altered swing without having to feel the pressure of anyone watching you. If you hit a few bad shots during these initial rounds, you will be able to quickly forget them knowing no one was there to witness. Once you have built up your confidence you can resume playing golf with others at your local course.

All golfers say they want to get better – but few are actually willing to do what it takes. The biggest hurdle in playing better golf is being willing to go outside of your comfort zone and use a swing that doesn't feel 'natural'.

As stated above, a swing without an over the top move is going to feel weird to a player who has been swinging over the top for years. If you are unwilling to make swings that feel uncomfortable for a while, you have no chance of ever-improving. Only players who make the choice to test their limits and try new techniques will be able to progress in the right direction.

If you struggle with an over the top move in your swing, you can rest assured that you aren't alone. This is one of the most common swing faults in the game, and countless players hit a slice because they are unable to solve it. Use the drills and instruction above to correct the error, and give yourself plenty of time on the practice range to make the necessary changes before taking your new slice-free swing back out onto the course.

❖ ❖ ❖

# CHAPTER 10: <u>TURN THE TIDE ON A BAD ROUND</u>

A n 18-hole round of golf is more like a marathon than a sprint. Every time you play, you'll encounter a stretch of shots or holes where nothing goes right and your score heads south. Don't let it take your mind with it.

Because in-round slumps can't be completely eliminated, the key is to limit their length and damage. Doing this means recognizing how you typically deal with on-course adversity.

Some players get angry, throw clubs and become so flustered they can barely see straight. Others head in the opposite direction, digging a deeper hole as they grow more and more dejected. In between these extremes lie emotionally neutral, analytical types, who remain poised while trying to figure out what's wrong with their swings.

Hotheads and gloomy Gusses have the hardest time halting a sudden slide. Studious detachment has its downside, too. Let's explore ways each personality type can better handle lapses on the golf course.

## The Hothead

Deep breath. OK, let's put things in perspective. You're playing golf here, not chasing criminals or trading billions of dollars in stock. Nothing that happens on the course will seriously affect your life, let alone anyone else's.

When you feel your temper starts to rise, pause, and take that big breath. Acknowledge the absurdity of getting so worked up over a silly game. Laugh at yourself, even if it's on the inside. Wiggle your fingers, lightly shake your arms, and gently rotate your neck to release tension.

Feel better? Good. Now forget your last slice or shank and focus on the next shot with a clear mind. If you slice it again, so what? It's not like you lost a million bucks on a bad trade. Besides, even the best golfers have bad holes – bad days, too.

Here's a chapter offering more tips for the temperamental golfer: Control Your Emotions, Control Your Game

## The Gloomy Gus

So you chunked one into the lake and sculled your next shot over the green. Guess what? It doesn't make you a bad person. It just means you're about to make a triple-bogey.

Like Mr. Hothead, our Gloomy Gus must find a proper perspective when his golf game sours. Instead of calming down, however, his way out requires perking up.

Lift your chin and drink in the beauty of your surroundings. Pretty nice, huh? Do a few jumping jacks or walk briskly to your ball to get the blood pumping. Now think about your most recent good shot or the best shot you've ever hit on the hole you're playing. Close your eyes and visualize repeating it this time. Then make it happen.

## The Professor

Rational types have the best chance of cutting a bad spell short. Being even-keeled, they're less susceptible to swing-killing tension of debilitating despair. Problem is, they often over-think and fall prey to "paralysis by analysis."

There's nothing wrong with breaking down your bad swings in search of an answer. But one faulty fix usually leads to another, sending you further down the rabbit hole. Before long, you've got three, four, or 10 swing thoughts in your head and you can't even draw the club back.

Instead of endlessly chasing a technical solution, try the most basic approach in golf: "See ball, hit the ball." It's as simple as it sounds. Banish all thoughts about the swing itself, focus on the back of the ball, and hit it.

There's no guarantee you'll like the results. But "see the ball, hit the ball" has remarkable swing-freeing powers that may well arrest your skid.

One final note that applies to all golfer types: Consider walking the course instead of riding a cart. When the inevitable bad spell strikes, the time and energy spent walking between shots helps Mr. Hothead calm down, helps Gloomy Gus cheer up, and gives The Professor a chance to sort through his thoughts.

## How to Turn the Tide on a Bad Round

When you head out to the course for a round on a busy Saturday morning, you will likely find the driving range filled with golfers getting ready to play. Most golfers like to at least hit a few balls before they head to the first tee, just to get warmed up and find a rhythm for their swing.

At this point, nearly every golfer on the range has the same goal for their round – to get off to a good start. They want to hit good shots on the first couple of holes, hopefully, make a couple of pars, and hit the ground running for the rest of the day.

Of course, this is desirable for obvious reasons, as you don't want to waste shots right at the start of your round. But what if you don't get off to a good start? What if you play poorly on the first couple of holes, even after a great warmup?

This is going to happen from time to time, unfortunately. No matter how focused you might be when you hit the first tee, it is still possible that you'll get off to a poor start. When that happens, you need to know how to turn the tide as quickly as possible.

In this chapter, we are going to offer some advice on how to turn around a bad round. This is something that challenges the average golfer on a regular basis, and it even gives professionals trouble from time to time.

Rather than being about your physical abilities, turning a bad round into a good round is all about your mental toughness. Sure, you might need to make a couple of physical tweaks to get things going – and we will discuss that later – but most of what you need to do is get your mind in the right place.

Once you learn how to turn the tide quickly on a bad round, you will find something interesting – many of your best rounds of golf actually start poorly. Some of the best rounds of golf that have ever been played in the professional game started with a bogey before the player got going and made plenty of birdies the rest of the way.

Don't make the mistake of thinking that you are destined to play a poor round just because you got off to a bad start. A great start doesn't guarantee that you are going to play a great round, and the opposite is true as well. Take each hole as an individual challenge and add them all up at the end of the day.

All of the content below is based on a right-handed golfer. If you happen to play left-handed, please take a moment to reverse the directions as necessary.

## The Basics

Right off the bat, we can identify a few basic tips that you can use to gain control over a bad round. The last thing you want to do is let your bad round spiral out of control to the point where you have played several poor holes in a row.

At that point, it might be too late to save a decent score for the day, despite your best efforts. So what can you do to 'right the ship' when things aren't going your way? Give these simple tips a try.

**Slow yourself down.** It is easy to fall into the trap of doing everything too quickly when you aren't playing well. You are probably frustrated with your poor play, and the body's natural reaction to frustration and anger is to speed up. Of course, as you already know, speeding up is certainly not going to help you play better golf.

Between holes, or even between shots if possible, take a moment to take a few deep breaths and slow yourself down. This can have a powerful effect on the way you play your next shot. Just by taking time to calm down and refocus on the task at hand, you might be able to bring your game back into shape without taking any other action.

**Use a conservative game plan.** This is one of the best steps you can take to get things back on track, yet few golfers ever are willing to make this adjustment. When you are playing poorly, you might be tempted to hit more aggressive shots in order to make up for the mistakes which are already reflected on your card.

This is the opposite of what you should be doing, however. When a round is going poorly, the correct response is to make your game plan more conservative in order to keep the ball in play and make it through some holes without any major damage. You obviously don't have your best game at the moment, so playing aggressively is only going to lead to trouble.

Use less club off the tee, aim for more conservative targets, and do your best to make a par or two. If you notice that your game starts to come around after a couple of conservative holes, you might have the necessary confidence and rhythm to play more aggressively once again.

**Avoid the temptation to change.** Common mistake golfers make when they get off to a bad start is to quickly change their swing technique. At the moment, it seems like this decision would make sense – if your current swing isn't working, why not try something else? This is faulty logic, however. Assuming you usually play at a higher level than you are on this day, there is no reason to think something is broken within your swing.

After all, that same swing has produced many good rounds in the past. So, the best bet is to stick with your technique and ride out this wave of poor play. Even professional golfers struggle from time to time, and they have highly refined swing techniques. If you make dramatic changes to your swing after a few poor holes, you will forever be searching for the right way to swing the club.

**Lean on your short game.** The fastest way to get out of trouble during a bad round is to play well in the short game. If you just aren't 'feeling it' with your full swing for one reason or another, focus intently on doing your best in the short game. Some golfers will actually give up a bit with regard to the short game during a bad round, thinking it doesn't matter since they aren't playing well anyway.

Nothing could be further from the truth. When your full swing is not holding up its end of the bargain, it is the job of the short game to come to the rescue. Focus on hitting quality chip shots and solid putts – you might be surprised to find that you can still find your way to a decent score through nothing more than some great short gameplay.

Each of the points listed above should be considered basics with regard to the challenge of turning around a bad day on the course. As you gain more and more experience playing golf, you will find that these tips come naturally.

For instance, when you feel yourself struggling, you might automatically start to pick safer targets as a way to keep your ball in play. Over the long run, your average score will come down if you can get better and better at making the best out of a bad round.

## It's All About Your Attitude

Let's get this out of the way right from the start – it's hard to have a good attitude on the course when you are playing poorly. We are going to talk about why it is important to stay positive, but you should note that we know it isn't easy.

You're going to feel frustrated, and you might even want to just give up for the day instead of pushing through to finish the round with the best possible score. Of course, just because something is difficult doesn't mean that you should give up. In fact, if you don't like difficult challenges, golf isn't the game for you.

To turn the tide on a bad round, the best ally you can have is a positive attitude. Instead of letting your negative mindset drag you further into poor play, you need to use your mind as a tool to get you back on track. This is easier said than done, but it is possible. To help you put the power of positive thinking on your side, we have identified some tips below.

**Remember positive experiences.** One of the simple steps you can take is to think back to some of your better rounds in the past. Remember great shots you hit or good scores you recorded on difficult courses. It shouldn't be hard to dig up these memories, as most golfers are able to easily recall their best shots and their best rounds.

You badly need a boost of confidence when you are in the middle of a poor round, and turning to positive memories can help to provide exactly that. Take a moment while someone else in your group is playing a shot to think back to a better round, then use that memory to provide some motivation and positivity for your next shot.

**Look at the scorecard.** Let's imagine for a second that you have played five holes of your current round, and you are off to a bad start. You have yet to make a par, and you have had a couple of terrible holes where you wasted several strokes. To say the least, things aren't going well. To keep your mind in a good place, take a moment to look at the scorecard.

However, you aren't going to look at the holes you have already played – you are going to look ahead at what's to come. Assuming you are playing 18 holes, there are still 13 of them left on which you can play well. Some of those are probably par fives, which usually represent scoring opportunities. Imagine all of the great shots you could hit over those final 13 holes if you just keep a positive attitude and give your best effort.

**Get competitive.** Sometimes, the only thing you need to keep yourself motivated is a little competitive edge. Do you want to lose badly to the other players in your group? Probably not.

Even if you can't recover all the way to beat them for the day, do your best to keep the scores as close as possible. It doesn't matter if you are playing for anything of value, this is all about pride and working hard to keep up with the other players around you.

A good attitude is important in golf, and that is certainly true when you get off to a bad start and need to turn things around quickly. You aren't going to get back on track unless you see things in a positive light, so do your best to think optimistically and avoid getting down on yourself. There will be time after the round to figure out why your game went wrong and what you can do to fix it – for now, the best thing you can do is be positive and enjoy the day.

◆ ◆ ◆

# CHAPTER 11: HIGH-PERCENTAGE SHOTS

I n basketball, the best teams tend to be those that get the easiest baskets. While their opponents are busy clanging 3-pointers off the rim, winning teams convert fast breaks into dunks and crisp passing into layups.

High-percentage shots are important in golf too. If you've ever heard a commentator mention that a pro had a "clean" round, that's what he's talking about. By hitting lots of fairways and greens, the golfer avoided trouble, gave himself opportunities for birdies, and strung together a series of no-sweat pars.

While your scoring goals may be less lofty, you can still make life easier on the course by playing the percentages. Doing that requires having a good grasp of your own abilities, a willingness to play within your limitations, the awareness to recognize when a cautious approach is your best bet, and the attentiveness to account for hazards and trouble spots.

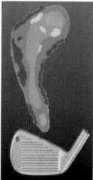

The first part, knowing what you're capable of, means having your club yardages down pat and owning a good sense of how well you play specific shots. For example, let's say your standard 8-iron flies 150 yards with a slight draw.

What do you do if faced with a pin tucked behind a bunker on the green's right side? The smart golfer takes the hazard out of play, aims for the center of the green, knocks it on, and either two-putts for an easy par or drains the birdie putt.

A golfer who doesn't heed his own shortcomings might take dead aim at the flag, put it in the sand and make bogey or worse. Don't be that golfer.

Sometimes, the seemingly bold or foolhardy shot plays into your hands. Using the same example, flip the flag to the green's left side, where it's guarded by a bunker. With your draw, all you've got to do is aim at the middle of the green and let your natural shot shape work the ball back to the pin. Your skill makes this a relatively low-risk approach.

Many players court big numbers when they fail to heed danger. How often do you "short-side" yourself on an approach shot, leaving little green to work with on a difficult chip? Instead of aggressively attacking a tucked flag, play to the fat of the green, two-putt, and stroll to the next tee.

Always play one shot ahead. On the tee, determine the best spot in the fairway from which to approach the green. From the fairway, find the safest place to chip or putt from and make that your "bail-out" area. Aim for the center of the green unless the pin is easily accessible.

Playing high-percentage golf doesn't mean playing timidly or with excess caution. It's all about recognizing opportunities and minimizing risk. Strive to play cleanly and you'll take a lot of the stress out of golf.

## How to Get High Percentage Golf Shots Driver to Putter

Golf, like any other sport, is a game that is played against an opponent. However, in golf, the opponent is not wearing a different jersey – instead, it is dressed in grass, sand, water, and more.

The course is your opponent in this great game, and your success or failure on the scorecard will be determined by how well you manage to attack your opponent. In addition to making quality swings and hitting good putts, you have to come up with a quality game plan if you are going to come out on top round after round.

Most golfers, when thinking about how to shoot lower scores, focus their attention only on the mechanics of their game. These players think that they will be able to lower their average score simply by making a better swing.

While a better swing will certainly help, mechanics alone will never take you to the golf 'promised land'. Instead, you have to pair those mechanics with some excellent strategy. When reliable swing fundamentals come together with a reliable on-course strategy, great things are possible.

In this chapter, we are going to focus exclusively on the strategic side of golf. Specifically, we are going to discuss how you can find a high percentage of golf shots all around the course. From the tee to the green, you should always be looking for high percentage shots in order to maximize your odds of success.

The golfer who finds the best opportunities throughout the day is likely to come out on top in the end, even if that is not the golfer with the best swing. Strategy can take you a long way in this game – but only when you think as much about course management as you do about the mechanics of your swing.

So what is a high percentage shot? To use a football analogy, a high percentage shot would be a short pass to a wide-open receiver. With no defenders in sight, the quarterback is highly likely to have success when throwing a short pass to his open receiver – and there is little that can go wrong.

Even if the pass is incomplete, it won't be intercepted because there are no defenders around. As compared to a long pass to a receiver covered by two defenders, the short pass to an open man is obviously the high percentage choice.

In golf, looking for high percentage shots means you are trying to tilt the odds of the game in your favor. No golfers execute their shots perfectly every time, so you always have to plan for the possibility of missing your target.

A high percentage shot would be one where you can make a mistake and still avoid serious trouble. Using a club that will keep you safely short of a water hazard, rather than trying to hit the ball all the way over the hazard, would be a safe play.

Most amateur golfers play far too aggressively from a course management standpoint, and they pay for that aggression on the scorecard. Playing high percentage golf might not be quite as exciting as taking on every tough shot, but it will pay off in the end when you see your scores come down.

All of the instruction below is based on a right-handed golfer. If you happen to play left-handed, please take a moment to reverse the directions as necessary.

## Analyzing Your Opponent

One of the great things about golf is the fact that no two courses are exactly alike. You can generally group courses into certain 'style' categories, but even within those categories, there is plenty of variation. For instance, some courses would be considered 'links-style', while others are 'parkland' or 'tree-lined'.

The general classification of a golf course might give you an idea of what you will face, but you can't know for sure until you see a course for yourself. They are all different, which is what makes golf such an interesting game to play for a lifetime.

To develop an appropriate strategy for any given round of golf, you need to carefully analyze the opponent you are going to face. Returning to our football analogy from earlier, a football coach would not finalize the game plan without thinking specifically about the team on the other side of the ball.

The strengths and weaknesses of the other team would be weighed, and the final plan for the game would be crafted based on how to best exploit the other team's weaknesses. By attacking the weaknesses and avoiding the strengths (as much as possible), a football team can give itself the best possible chance to win.

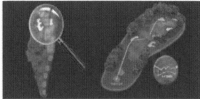

The story is the same in golf. When you play any course, your goal should be to attack the weaknesses of the course while staying away from its strengths. This will mean different things on different courses.

For instance, a course with narrow fairways but a short overall yardage will require you to place an emphasis on control. On such a course, you could hit irons off the tee to exploit the fact that there isn't a significant distance to be covered. You would be playing away from the problem of narrow fairways, therefore taking away the 'strength' of the course.

On the other hand, the opposite game plan would likely be the best bet when playing a long, wide-open golf course. This kind, of course, is a perfect opportunity to put your driver to work, as your errant drives are unlikely to be punished in any significant way. Your driver can help you cover the distance needed to attack the greens, so the challenge of playing a long course will be mitigated by the fact that you are hitting your longest club as often as possible.

The two examples in the previous paragraphs are oversimplifications, of course, but they make an important point. Anytime you face a new golf course, it is your job to identify what it is that makes the course difficult, and what it is that makes the course playable.

From there, you create a game plan which is designed to give yourself the best possible chance for success. Just as a football team would throw a lot of passes against a team with a poor passing defense, you should do whatever you can to exploit the weaknesses of the golf courses you face.

As you gain experience in this game, you will get better and better at the job of analyzing the golf course in front of you. At first, you might struggle to find ways to attack some courses, but nearly every course has weaknesses if you are willing to look hard enough.

Of course, it is important to match up your game plan with not only the design of the course but also with your own abilities. You shouldn't be trying to hit shots that you are not capable of hitting, so always keep your strategy within the realm of what you can do with a golf ball.

## Examples of High Percentage Shots

Although you are going to have a different game plan for each course you face, there are some types of high percentage shots which you should be looking for over and over again. These shots are available on many different golf courses, so you should always be on the lookout for a chance to use these plays. If you can get comfortable with each of the shots in the list below, you will always have some reliable safe options at your disposal.

**The tee shot short of the trouble.** Most par fours and fives have some form of trouble waiting to catch an errant tee shot. Sometimes, the trouble will be in the form of a water hazard, or even out of bounds stakes.

Other times, the trouble will be more subtle, like a fairway bunker or even a deep patch of rough. Whatever the case, you obviously want to keep your ball out of these areas. Rather than taking on the trouble and hoping to hit an accurate drive, you can choose to simply lay up short of the problem spots.

This strategy will leave you with a longer approach shot, but it will take the trouble completely out of play. You can't hit the ball into a water hazard if you can't reach the water with the club you have decided to use. It takes patience to use this type of high percentage play, but you will often be rewarded in the end.

**The approach shot to the wide side of the green.** This is perhaps the type of high percentage shot that could benefit the average amateur golfer the most. For most golfers, the process of picking a target for an approach shot involves taking aim at the flag at swinging away.

The problem with this method, of course, is the risk that you will be taking on in some cases when you aim directly at the flag. Rather than always aiming at the flag, you should consider playing away toward the wide side of the green in many cases.

By taking the high percentage option of hitting towards the big part of the green, you will hit more greens in regulation and you will have more birdie putts. Countless golfers could immediately take strokes off of their average score if they were simply willing to play away from the hole on many approach shots.

**Play into the big part of the dogleg.** When facing a tee shot to a fairway with a significant dogleg, you may be tempted to cut off the corner of the dogleg in order to get closer to the green for your second shot.

However, if you take on this aggressive line, you will be incurring a good deal of risk at the same time. By missing your line just slightly on such an aggressive tee shot, you could place your ball in serious trouble. On the other hand, you could give yourself a great chance of finding the fairway if you play to the big side of the dogleg.

For instance, if the hole is turning from left to right, consider playing down the left side to maximize your margin for error. Sure, you will be leaving a slightly longer approach shot, but that approach shot should be coming from the fairway.

**Lay up with the second shot on a par five.** It is certainly exciting to go for the green in two on a par five. However, once that excitement wears off, you may find that you have hit your ball into an undesirable location by trying to reach the green. In most cases, laying your ball up with the second shot is going to be the better choice.

This high percentage play will leave you with an easy third shot into the green, so you still may be able to record a birdie even after taking the lay-up option. Most par-five holes are designed with some sort of lay-up area available, so you shouldn't have much trouble finding a landing spot for this kind of play. You can go for par five greens in two from time to time when you have a realistic opportunity, but laying up is typically the higher percentage choice.

Depending on the kind of golf course you play, there will likely be other high percentage shots available to you throughout the day. In the end, it is going to be up to you to spot these options and then take advantage of them successfully with a good swing. By advancing your ball toward the target without taking on undue risk, you can keep your scorecard clean and your round on track.

## Finding the Right Positions

Sometimes, you need to take what the golf course is giving you in terms of high percentage shots. On other occasions, however, it is up to you to create those high percentage shots. By thinking a shot ahead – or even two shots ahead, in some cases – you can position your ball to leave yourself with a higher percentage shot for your next stroke. This kind of advanced strategy requires patience and careful thinking while on the course, but it offers you the opportunity to take your game to a new level.

Thinking at least one shot ahead is something professional golfers do on every single hole they play. To highlight this concept, we can come back to our football analogy one more time. For a football team, the goal is to pick up first downs all the way down the field until it becomes reasonable to go for the end zone (or to kick a field goal).

However, with four downs to work with, the team doesn't have to try for a first down on every single play. Instead, they can choose to run a play that will only pick up a few yards, in order to set up another play that can convert the first down. This takes patience, but it increases the odds of success in the long run.

To play good golf, you need to think like a football team. You don't have to hit the perfect shot with the swing you are currently making, but you do need to set yourself up to hit a great shot on your next attempt. How do you accomplish this goal? The following points are ways in which you can position yourself for success.

**Playing to the low side of the hole.** One of the basics of positioning your ball around the course is trying to find the low side of the hole whenever possible. Playing uphill is almost always easier than playing downhill as far as the short game is concerned, so you need to look for opportunities to place your ball in a spot that is lower than the hole.

For instance, if the green is sloped from back to front, leaving your ball short of the hole would be ideal. Professional golfers are constantly trying to keep the ball below the cup, and you should be following that lead.

**Picking the correct side to favor your ball flight.** The way you position your tee shots in the fairway should be related to the ball flight you tend to use for approach shots. A player who likes to hit a draw into the green will want to favor the left side of the fairway in order to provide enough room for that draw to work.

Likewise, a player who likes to fade his or her approach shots will want to find the right side of the fairway most of the time. Picture the type of approach shot you want to hit into the green and then do your best to position your ball to facilitate such a play.

**Avoiding a scary shot.** Don't like to have to carry your ball a long distance over water? Rather than having to face such a proposition, do your best to avoid that kind of situation in the first place. All golfers have their own personal 'fears' when it comes to various types of shots that they don't want to play.

There is no shame in doing your best to hide from these fears – there are no points for bravery awarded in golf. Your only goal is to get around the course in as few strokes as possible, so plan your way around situations which make you uncomfortable.

**Playing unconventional golf.** Sometimes, playing to the percentages will mean taking an unconventional path to the hole. For example, you might decide to lay up with your second shot on a par four. Or, you might even decide to lay up off the tee on a long par three.

You should not feel compelled to play a shot in a particular way just because the conventions of golf say it should be so. Again, the goal is the lowest score possible, and achieving that score might require thinking outside the box from time to time.

Your job as a golfer is to put yourself in the best possible positions to succeed. You want to find as many high percentage shots as you can, and those situations are not always going to be presented to you on a platter. Many times, you will have to earn your high percentage shot by making a smart decision on the previous swing.

## Bringing Your Patience

The word patience has been mentioned a few times in this chapter, and for good reason. When playing a style of golf which is based largely on turning the percentages in your favor, you are going to need to bring plenty of patience along for the ride. It is easy to lose your patience in this frustrating game, but you cannot afford to go down that road if you want to post a good score at the end of the day.

To do a good job of maintaining your patience from start to finish, it is important to stick with a reliable pre-shot routine. A good pre-shot routine can help you to let go of the frustration you may be feeling from a previous shot before you get on with your next swing.

Also, the time you take to complete your pre-shot routine can include a moment dedicated to thinking about your strategy. It will take practice to learn how to stay patient for an entire round of golf, but reaching this goal is a great way to raise the level of your game.

Golf is as much mental as it is physical when it comes to posting a good score. Making nice swings will help you navigate the course, but those swings need to be accompanied by some solid decision making.

Putting yourself in a position to play high percentage shots throughout most of the round is going to cause your stress levels to go down – and your scores should go down at the same time. There are plenty of high percentage shots to find on the course, as long as you know where to look.

# CHAPTER 12: WORK THE BALL

T he ability to "work" the golf ball is one key difference between average golfers and low-handicappers. To "work" the ball means to intentionally hit shots that curve in one direction or the other, to play shots with extra height or keep the ball low when needed, and generally control the spin, trajectory, and shape of your shots.

It's advanced stuff but within every golfer's grasp. And no matter your current skill level, being able to work the ball in at least one direction can pay big dividends.

Before learning the technique needed to play these specialty shots, you must understand what causes the ball to curve in mid-air. This tutorial provides the easy-to-understand basics of sidespin:

**What Makes the Golf Ball Curve?**

Now let's apply this knowledge to the setup and swing techniques used to play the four standard shots in every shotmaker's repertoire: The fade, the draw, the high shot, and the low shot. (Descriptions are for right-handed golfers).

**Fade (soft left-to-right curve):** The fade is your go-to shot off the tee of most par 4 and par 5 holes that dogleg to the right. A fade will follow the bend of the fairway, giving you a better chance of hitting and holding the short grass. The fade is also handy for playing approach shots when the flag is located on the green's right side.

Set up for a fade by aiming the clubface at the target – the spot where you want the ball to finish.

Place your feet slightly open (aligned left) in relation to the clubface. The shoulders and hips should line up with your feet.

Your swing should follow the alignment of your body, on a path left of the target.

You may find it helpful to stand a little closer to the ball, creating a more upright swing plane, and to keep the back of your left hand pointed at the target through impact. This prevents the right hand from rolling over the left, closing the clubface too soon, and eliminating the left-to-right sidespin which generates a fade.

**Draw (soft right-to-left curve):** The opposite of a fade, use the draw on dogleg-left holes and to reach pins on the green's left side.

**To hit a draw, simply flip the instructions for a fade:**

Set up by aiming the clubface at the target.

Place your feet slightly closed (aligned right) in relation to the clubface. The shoulders and hips are in line with your feet.

Swing along your body line, right of the target.

Standing a few inches farther from the ball will create a flatter swing plane more conducive to hitting a draw. Also, focus on rolling the right hand over the left through the impact zone to impart the proper sidespin.

**High shot:** There are numerous instances where it's helpful to launch the ball very high in the air – hitting over trees, trying to stop an iron shot on a small portion of the green, or when you're looking to take advantage of a tailwind for extra distance.

There's nothing complicated about the physics here. Hitting the ball high means utilizing as much of the club's loft as possible.

Set up with the ball slightly forward of its normal position for the club you're using. For example, if it's a 6-iron, play it about an inch to the left of your usual ball position.

Make sure the hands aren't too far ahead of the ball as this will effectively reduce the club's loft.

If the situation allows, open your stance, and play a fade. Fades fly higher and land more softly than draws or straight shots.

In addition, stand closer to the ball and concentrate on finishing the swing with your hands high overhead. (Think "high shot, high finish.")

**Low shot:** Need to hit the ball beneath tree branches, keeping it down when playing into a headwind, or run the ball onto the green? Follow these rules for hitting it low.

At address, the ball should be farther back (to the right) in your stance than normal.

Set your hands well ahead of the ball to deloft the club.

A mild draw often works well on low shots. Close the clubface or your stance to add sidespin.

By standing a bit farther from the ball, you'll create a more rounded swing plane that promotes a low, drawing shot. Finish with your hands at or below shoulder height. (Think "low shot, low finish.")

There you have it – Working the Ball 101. Your setup is the most important element in controlling shots and bending the ball to your will. Master the fundamentals and enjoy the perks that come with being a genuine shotmaker.

## How to Work the Golf Ball

In golf, 'working the ball' is the act of intentionally curving your shots in one direction or another. For example, if you are playing a hole that has a dogleg to the left, you could 'work' your shot from right to left in order to fit the ball into the fairway.

While working the ball is something that is seen regularly on the PGA Tour, very few amateur golfers even try to work their shots – and even fewer succeed. It is not easy to accurately work the ball into your targets, but it can be very rewarding when executed correctly. By taking the time and effort on the practice range to learn how to work the ball, you will be greatly increasing your chances of shooting good scores out on the course.

One mistake that is made by most amateur golfers is assuming that they aren't good enough to try working the ball from time to time. It doesn't matter what level of golfer you are at the moment, you should always be open to the idea of trying to learn new skills. Even if your standard swing is inconsistent and ineffective most of the time, you can still work on the basics of working the ball.

This kind of practice can benefit you because not only will you learn how to create some different shot shapes, but you will also learn a lot about your standard swing. You just might be surprised at how much your normal swing can improve when you decide to alter it slightly in the pursuit of new trajectories.

You don't have to work the ball on every shot in order for this skill to add value to your game. In fact, you will probably only want to work the ball a few times per round, if even that many. Most of the time, your standard shot shape will be appropriate for the hole that is in front of you.

Since your standard shot is the one that you hit most consistently, sticking with it as frequently as possible makes sense. Only change your ball flight on the course when it is truly necessary to get your ball close to the target. A big part of the challenge in this area of golf is not only learning how to work the golf ball, but also understanding when the time is right to deploy this new skill.

The golf ball that you play will also have a say in how much you are able to work the golf ball around the course. To work the ball successfully, you need a ball that is able to spin sufficiently to curve in one direction or the other. If you are using a 'hard' golf ball (usually a low-priced model), you might not be able to get enough spin to really work the ball any significant amount. Once you have learned the basic skills involved with working the golf ball, make sure that you are using a ball which will allow you to put your new talents to use.

All of the instruction contained below is based on a right-handed golfer. If you happen to play left-handed, please be sure to reverse the directions as necessary.

## *Your Basic Swing Doesn't Change*

Learning to work the golf ball doesn't mean you need to learn an entirely new golf swing. In fact, it means quite the opposite. You want to use your regular golf swing – with only some minor modifications – in order to alter your ball flight as desired. By keeping your swing as close to normal as possible, you will make it easier to strike the ball cleanly time after time.

Making radical changes to your swing technique on the fly is never going to be a successful strategy, so don't even try it. Start from your basic swinging motion and subtly change how you move the club until you are able to bend the ball in a variety of directions.

There are three basic ways in which you can alter your swing technique in order to work the ball around the course. Each of them can be effective on their own, although you may have to combine two or even all three if you want to achieve dramatic results.

**Change Your Stance.** This is probably the most common method used to work the golf ball. By altering your stance slightly, you can change the path of the club during the swing – and you will then change the spin that is put on the ball as a result. For example, if you wish to hit a right to left hooking ball flight, you will simply close your stance relative to the target line and make your usual swing.

Hopefully, the clubhead will follow the path of your stance, and it will move through impact from inside to out – meaning the ball will receive hook spin. To do the opposite and create a fade, your stance would need to be open to the target line. For many people, adjusting the stance at address is the only change that will be necessary in order to work the ball.

**Change Your Grip.** Altering your grip at address to work the ball is an advanced skill, but it can give you a valuable bit of control over your ball flight. Unlike changing your stance, which can dramatically affect your ball flight, changing your grip should be used to make subtle tweaks to the path of the ball in the air.

For instance, imagine you normally hit a slight fade with your standard swing. If you would like to hit a small draw for a particular shot, you could simply strengthen your left-hand grip and then make your usual swinging motion. The path of your club will be the same as always, but the ball should turn over to the left thanks to your stronger grip.

To encourage a fade instead of a draw, you would weaken your grip slightly. Again, this is not meant to be a radical adjustment, but rather one that can be used to gently change the trajectory of the ball.

**Change Your Ball Position.** Working the ball can come down to something as simple as changing your ball position prior to the swing. If you wish to work a lower shot in toward the target, play the ball back in your stance. Want to hit it higher? Move the ball forward and give the club time to fully release prior to impact.

Also, moving the ball back will promote a draw while playing it forward will encourage a fade. Experiment with different ball positions on the driving range to determine exactly what they do to your ball flight.

It is important to avoid making drastic swing changes any time you want to work the golf ball. The last thing you want to do is ruin your regular swing technique while trying to hit a few curved shots, so be careful when altering your stance, grip, or ball position. Only make these changes when necessary to hit a certain shot, and go right back to your usual technique on the next 'standard' shot that you face.

## The Challenge of Practicing on the Range

When you decide to learn how to work the ball, your first step will likely be to head to the practice range. There is nothing wrong with that idea necessarily, but it does come with a significant downside – range balls don't behave like a normal golf ball does as they fly through the air.

Range balls are designed for longevity rather than performance, so they are typically made with a hardcover that spins very little. The balls that you hit on the range are unlikely to perform anything like the balls you have in your bag, so the benefit of your practice sessions will be limited. You may think you have learned how to work the ball nicely on the range only to find that your techniques aren't really working at all out on the course.

The best way to go about learning how to work the ball is to practice your mechanics on the range while mostly ignoring the results of the ball flight. You can watch the ball fly through the air, but don't put too much stock in the trajectory that you are seeing in front of you. After you have spent a little bit of time learning the basic techniques like adjusting your stance and your grip, take your new shots out onto the course to test them under real conditions.

By working the ball a few times during a casual round of golf, you will start to see the effects of your practice sessions. It will take some time to gain a reasonable amount of control over these shots, but you are only going to learn that control while using a real golf ball.

It is tempting to play for your best score every time you hit the course, but playing a few casual rounds from time to time where you don't worry about the scorecard can be great for your game.

If you get the chance, schedule a round sometime soon where you go out by yourself and simply work on hitting new shots. You don't even need to keep score – just challenge yourself to try new shots so you can see what works and what doesn't. Once you break free from the idea of keeping score on every hole, you might be surprised to learn how much fun it can be to play this kind of golf.

You will feel more relaxed than you do when playing for a score, and you will be able to let your natural ability come through. When you do come back to the course to play a normal round focused on shooting a good score, you will have learned some lessons and hopefully discovered some new shots that can help you play your best.

It is important to note that you shouldn't ditch the driving range entirely, despite its limitations. No, you aren't going to learn much about your ball flight on the range, but you can still sharpen the mechanics of your swing and make yourself more consistent before you head onto the course.

Repetitions are crucial when trying to improve your technique, so feel free to visit the range regularly. As long as you don't expect to see the same ball flight on the course as you do on the range, you can still gain a nice benefit from your time spent on the practice tee.

## Knowing When to Work the Ball

Even after you have learned how to work the ball through a period of trial and error on the golf course, you will still have to learn how to apply your new skills properly. It would be a huge mistake to try working the ball in various directions on each shot that you hit – that would lead to wild inconsistency and frustrating results.

At the same time, there is no point in learning a new skill if you are never going to take it out of the bag. The ability to pick and choose your spots is the big key when it comes to proper use of working the ball.

The following list includes a variety of situations when it would be acceptable to work the ball in order to get closer to your target.

Dogleg Left    Dogleg Right

**Get Around a Big Dogleg.** On a course that has plenty of trees guarding dogleg fairways, you might have no choice but to attempt to work the ball around a corner in order to find the short grass. Hitting the fairway should always be a priority, even if that means going for one of your 'specialty' shots to do so.

Take a look at the fairway in front of you and decide if your normal shot can fit the hole as it is laid out, or you will need to work the ball. Only when you really need to work a specific shot into the fairway should you attempt to do so.

Even then, don't attempt anything too risky if there is water or out of bounds guarding the hole. Keeping your ball in play is always the top priority, so pick the option that gives you the best chance at avoiding penalty shots while moving toward the green.

**Limiting the Effect of the Wind.** Playing golf is the wind is always a challenge. During the round, you are sure to face a number of uncomfortable shots that require you to rise to the occasion in order to hit the target. If playing on a windy day, you might find the need to work the ball into the breeze to keep it online.

For example, if you are playing a hole where the wind is blowing hard from left to right, you might want to work a draw into that wind to counteract its effects. If you didn't choose to play a draw, you would be forced to aim out to the left and let your ball ride the wind – which is always a difficult option to get just right.

**When You Need to Hit It Close.** If it is getting late in your round and you absolutely need a birdie to shoot your goal score or beat your playing partner, go ahead and work the ball in an attempt to get as close to the hole as possible.

You might not be able to hit your standard shot and get close to a hole on the far right of the green, for example, but you could maybe work a fade in there to set up a birdie putt. This isn't the kind of strategy that you want to use all throughout a round, but there is a certain point where it makes sense to 'go for broke'.

**Avoid a Big Hazard.** As mentioned above, keeping your ball away from major hazards is a big part of shooting a good score. To that end, you can use your skills in working the golf ball to steer clear of things like water hazards and out of bounds stakes. When standing on the tee of a long par four with out of bounds right, for instance, feel free to set up for your draw in order to keep the ball well away from the trouble.

Even if you miss in the left rough, you should still have a play toward the green – and you will be much better off than had you blasted the ball out of bounds. There is nothing wrong with playing smart and curving the ball away from trouble from time to time, even if that means taking a conservative path.

As you gain experience working the ball around the course, you will get a better understanding of when you should use this skill, and when you should keep it in the bag. A round of golf is a non-stop barrage of decisions that have to be made one after another. The player who makes the best decisions, and then is able to execute on those decisions, is the one who will come out on top.

## Finding the Right Golf Ball

Playing the proper golf ball is a big part of this equation. If you don't have the right ball on the ground in front of you, it really doesn't matter how much you practice – you aren't going to be able to work the ball as you wish. So what is the right golf ball for you? That is a question that no one else can answer for you.

It is important that you test out a variety of golf balls until you find the one that proves the right amount of spin – both backspin and sidespin – when coming off your club. Spin rates with specific golf balls can vary wildly from player to player, so you can't just look at the results for other golfers and assume that they will apply to you as well.

If you are playing a golf ball that doesn't spin enough, you won't be able to work the ball successfully. Instead, the ball will fly mostly straight on the majority of your shots, unless you make a particularly bad swing that sends the ball curving dramatically to the left or right.

On the other hand, a ball with a spin rate that is too high for your game could fly far offline even when you make a pretty good swing. If you are going to have success working the ball while maintaining control over your standard shots at the same time, you need to find the ball that strikes a perfect balance.

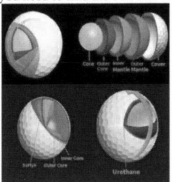

It should be noted that you don't necessarily have to play the most expensive ball on the market to have success working your shots. While the high-end golf balls typically do offer the biggest spin rate, you can still work shots with a less-expensive model that matches your swing nicely.

As you are learning how to work the ball, try acquiring a few different golf balls models that you can test out on the course. Rotate through the various options and you should quickly find which ones perform well for your swing, and which ones don't. Consistency is a good thing on the golf course when you can find it, so try to stick with one model of golf ball once you locate a brand that performs well coming off your clubs.

Working the golf ball is a skill that doesn't have to be limited to just the best players in the world. In fact, all golfers can try to work the ball to some degree, as learning how to turn the ball right and left can help you become a better overall player.

Feel free to work on your skills on the driving range, but remember that the ball flights you see on the range aren't necessarily reflective of what will happen on the course. Add new shots to your bag, while keeping your standard shots in place, and you can lower your scores by being better equipped to handle everything the course throws at you.

# CHAPTER 13: <u>TOOL FOR CREATING</u> <u>CLUBHEAD LAG</u>

D o you unleash the golf club into the ball with a flash of accelerating speed? Or do your shots produce a weak sound and fly with rapidly diminishing velocity?

In short, does your golf swing make an impact? If not, an impact bag could make you a more powerful player.

Available online and through golf retail outlets, impact bags are medium-sized cushions designed to be hit with a golf club. (A bean bag chair, a garbage bag filled with towels, or any similar object can serve the same purpose.) Practicing with an impact bag is the most widely recommended method for increasing your clubhead lag, also called a "late release."

Lag is created when the angle between the left arm and shaft is retained from the top of the swing into the downswing. Some golfers, like Sergio Garcia, manage to tighten this angle on the way down, generating an extremely powerful punch as the wrists and hands unwind into the ball.

Now for the impact bag. It's a great tool for golf drills that train specific movements, but which would be difficult to perform by hitting a golf ball. In fact, hitting a bag causes golfers to naturally drive into the impact zone using their whole body, rather than throwing the hands and wrists at it.

Working with a bag will ingrain a swing in which the hands lead the clubhead to contact – the key to compressing the ball against the turf with your irons and generating clubhead speed with the driver.

**Here's a basic drill to get you started with an impact bag or suitable substitute:**

Using a short or mid-iron, set up with the back edge of the bag in the middle of your stance, the shaft and clubhead touching the bag.

Move your hands toward the target, with the shaft pressing into the bag and leaning forward. Turn your hips slightly left with the shoulders square to the target. This is the position you want at impact.

Make a few short swings where you take the club back to hip height, then return it to the impact position described above. Slowly rotate your hips left of the target as the club makes contact.

Make progressively longer swings, always leading the downswing with your hips and keeping the hands ahead of the clubhead.

This is a good drill to use regularly to maintain a sense of the correct impact position.

## Impact Bag Great Tool for Creating Clubhead Lag

When you think about golf equipment, you probably think about things like clubs, balls, shoes, and more. However, the category of golf 'equipment' can also carry over into training gear, as having a couple of good pieces of training equipment can be a big help in your pursuit of becoming a better player.

Fortunately, there are a number of training items that can be added to your collection for a relatively minor financial investment. You don't need to buy all of the golf practice equipment on the market, but choosing a key piece or two that you can use during your range sessions will be highly beneficial.

One of the pieces of practice equipment that you should consider is an impact bag. An impact bag is a relatively soft bag that can be used to check on your impact position at the bottom of the swing. The way it works is quite simple – you make your swing, strike the bag, and the club (and your body) stops in place at the bottom.

Now that you are 'frozen' in your impact position, you can check on your technique to look for any points that need improvement. You shouldn't go full out into an impact bag, as you could damage your club or hurt yourself, but using one with less-than-full swings to check on your mechanics is a method many golfers have used over the years.

In this chapter, we are going to cover the idea of using an impact bag to learn how to lag the clubhead successfully. Lag is a concept that escapes many amateur golfers, which is why they usually aren't able to hit the ball as far as their professional counterparts.

The ability to lag the clubhead is one of the most important skills you can have as a ball-striker since lag leads to both increase clubhead speed and improved quality of contact. In golf terms, the word 'lag' refers to the clubhead trailing behind the hands during the downswing.

Ideally, your hands will lead the way coming down into the ball, with the clubhead only releasing through impact after the hands have arrived at the bottom. Of course, the average golfer fails to achieve lag in the downswing, instead of allowing the clubhead to lead the way with the hands trailing behind. If you can flip this around and install some lag in your swing, you will notice an immediate boost in the power that you are capable of achieving.

Before you get started working on this concept, it is important to understand one thing – lag is a difficult concept to grasp for many players, and it is even harder to put it into your swing. If you are a player who is used to hitting the ball without lag, you are going to have to put in plenty of practice time before you will be able to execute a swing which includes lag.

The added power in your swing might be immediate when you figure out lag, but it is going to take some time and plenty of practice balls before you can iron out your ball flight and use this swing effectively on the course.

All of the content below is based on a right-handed golfer. If you happen to play left-handed, please take a moment to reverse the directions as necessary.

## How Lag Is Created

Before getting to the impact bag portion of this task, we are first going to review what it is that you need to do in a golf swing in order to create lag. Specifically, there are three points that must be checked off if you are going to lag the club into the ball consistently swing after swing. Nearly every professional golfer that you see on TV is able to check off these points, and you should work hard to be able to say the same.

The following are the three keys that are required if you are going to lag the club nicely in your downswing.

**Set the club in the backswing.** One of the main points that need to be understood when it comes to lagging the club on the way down is that you have to set it on the way back. To 'set' the club in your backswing means to hinge your wrists into a position where the shaft of the club and your left forearm form a 90* angle.

Some players like to get this set out of the way early in the backswing, while others prefer to wait until they are almost all the way to the top before setting the club. It doesn't particularly matter when you do the set – as long as it gets done.

Many amateurs never set the club at all going back, and therefore they have no chance to lag the club coming down. Before you even consider working with an impact bag to learn lag in the downswing, make sure you are setting the club nicely in your backswing.

**Strong left-hand grip**. It is the left hand that is going to largely determine how well you are able to lag the club coming down into impact. You need to have a comfortable but firm grip on the club with your left hand, while your right can remain more relaxed throughout much of the swing.

The left hand is going to pull the club down into the slot early in the downswing, and then it is going to lead the way into impact before the release begins to take over. If you are going to be able to reach a point where lag is an important part of your swing, you are going to have to be confident in the grip that your left hand has at the end of the club.

**Great lower body turn.** Think of your lower body as the engine that drives the downswing forward through the ball. While you need your left hand to perform on the way down if you are going to strike the ball with great lag, you also need the rotation of your lower body to build speed successfully.

Start the downswing by turning your left hip toward the target and keep that rotation going all the way through. Many golfers don't believe that the lower body could actually have anything to do with lagging the club behind their hands, but everything in the golf swing is connected. All of the world's top golfers are great at using their lower bodies as a speed generator, and you should make it a goal to do the same.

There is a lot to think about when it comes to the idea of lag, so it is best to go through the three points above one at a time. Are you setting the club nicely in the backswing? If so, that is one point that you can check off of the list. Is your left hand doing its job, and are your hips turning through toward the target? If all of these answers are a 'yes', you should be well on your way to a powerful downswing that has plenty of lag to launch the ball off into the distance.

## Ideal Impact Position

To evaluate the position that you achieve when using an impact bag, you should first have a clear picture of what an ideal impact position will look like for the swing you want to make. If you are hoping to lag the club, there are some specific positions that your body needs to find at the bottom of the swing.

The list below includes three positions that you should strive to hit when you reach impact – once you start using the impact bag, you can refer back to this list as you are determining what (if any) changes need to be made to your technique.

**Hands over the ball.** This is the first thing you should look for when checking on your impact position with regard to lag. Your hands should be over the ball, or slightly in front of the ball (closer to the target) when you make contact.

Unfortunately, this is where so many players go wrong. Instead of having the hands over the ball or beyond, the average player has their hands behind the ball at impact – which leads to weak contact and off-line shots.

Checking your impact position is the best way to confirm that you have actually lagged the club on the way down. If your hands are over the ball or slightly beyond, you can be confident that lag has taken place.

**Right heel off of the ground.** This point is a great indication that your lower body has done its job in the downswing. As you turn your hips aggressively toward the target on the way down, your right foot should begin to gradually come up off the ground. At impact, you should find that your right heel has come up slightly off of the turf, while your toes are still firmly planted on the ground.

If you notice that your right heel is not coming off the ground at all by the time you reach impact, there is a good chance that your lower body is not doing its job correctly. Work on engaging your hips right from the beginning of the downswing and you should see that right heel begins to work its way off the ground by the time you make contact.

**Eyes on the ball.** Whether you are working on lag or anything else in your swing, it is always important to keep your eyes on the ball throughout the swing. As it relates to lag specifically, keeping your head down will permit your lower body rotation to continue on through the swing – which is essential for ball striking success.

If you let your eyes and head come up out of the swing early, your lower body rotation will likely stop and you will make a weak pass at the ball through impact. Pick out a specific spot on the top of the ball and make that your focus until after the strike has been made.

Using an impact bag is a great way to freeze your impact position so that it can be accurately evaluated – but that will only be helpful if you have a clear picture in your mind of what you need to achieve. Review the three points above and then check to see if you are hitting each of them when you actually start using the impact bag during your practice sessions.

## Impact Bag Practice

Now that we have reviewed the various technical details involved with lag and how it is created, it is time to go over how you can use an impact bag to improve your technique. Obviously, the first step in this process is to acquire an impact bag to add to your collection of golf equipment.

There are a number of quality impact bags available today, and you can find them online as well as in your local golf shops. This probably isn't a piece of gear that you will want to carry with you on a regular basis when you head to the course, so you should plan on simply packing it up to take on days when you intend to use it.

With your impact bag along for the trip and your spot on the range staked out, set the bag in front of you and follow the steps below to use it successfully.

To start, take one of your short irons from the bag. You can use pretty much any of your irons for this drill, but it is best to start with something like a pitching wedge. Try to avoid using any graphite shafted clubs with your impact bag, as they may be a little more susceptible to damage than the steel shafted models you carry. Of course, since you will be striking the impact bag at the bottom of the swing, you aren't going to need any golf balls at this time.

Position the impact bag on the ground in front of you in the same position that the ball would occupy if you were hitting a normal shot. As you take your stance, make sure you do everything that you would do before any other swing – go through your pre-shot routine, pick out a target, settle into your stance, and do anything else that you usually do to get comfortable. If this drill is going to be effective, it needs to mirror your normal process as closely as possible.

When you are ready to take a swing, your goal is going to be to make your full swing while only using about a quarter of your normal speed. Shortening your swing in order to take the speed out of it really won't accomplish the goal, because a shorter swing isn't going to tell you anything about your full swing impact position.

Instead, go ahead and use your full swinging motion while only applying about 25% of your usual effort. It is important to make sure that you aren't swinging too hard when using your impact bag, or injury could result (or damage to the club). Start out moving extremely slow in your swing and gradually pick up the pace until you find a speed that is safe to use with the bag while still giving you the feedback you need.

As you get to the bottom of the swing, the club is going to run into the impact bag – and it should stop cold as a result. When the club does stop, it is important that you hold your position throughout your body so you can analyze the results. If you let yourself move quickly after making contact with the bag, you won't be able to get a good read on your actual impact position.

Now that you are holding your impact position after make a slow-speed full swing, you can look over the positions that your body is in and decide how you have done. Are your hands over the bag, or slightly in front of the position where the ball would be? Is your right heel up off the ground? Check on these important points to find out if your swing technique is allowing you to lag the club properly.

The nice thing about using an impact bag for a practice session is that the bag isn't going anywhere – you can hit it again and again, as many times as you would like. Unlike a bucket of balls that you buy at the range, the impact bag isn't going to run out after a number of swings.

Remember, it is crucial that you don't hit the bag too hard, as you would be running the risk of damaging your clubs or yourself. Take it very slow at first, work your way up to a safe and comfortable speed (which will still be nowhere near your regular full swing), and learn from what you are finding in your impact position as the club is stopped by the bag.

## *The Benefits of Lag*

When most people think about adding lag to their swing, they think about the distance that can be gained. It is true – you can certainly add yardage to your shots by learning how to lag the club. However, the distance benefits are only one part of the equation.

Lagging the club in the downswing will actually help you in a number of different ways, making you a better ball striker all the way around. If you need any further encouragement to decide to work on your lag with the help of an impact bag, review the following non-power benefits to creating great lag.

**Clean strike.** Hitting the ball cleanly should always be one of your main goals when you stand over the ball, and you will hit more shots cleanly when you are able to use lag. The way your body has to move in the swing to create lag will lead to more consistent delivery of the club to the back of the ball, as compared to a swing that uses the hands early in the action. It might take some time and practice to sharpen up your ball-striking with the use of lag, but the end result could be some of the best shots of your life.

**Get out of the rough.** A lagging downswing will usually create a steeper angle of attack than what you would see in a swing without lag. With that steep angle of attack, you should be able to miss some of the long grass behind your ball when playing from the rough. It is the grass that gets stuck between your club and the ball that causes your shots from the rough to frequently come up short of the target, but you can minimize that problem when you use plenty of lag on the way down. If you are a golfer who typically has a lot of trouble with the long grass, lag is one of the best ways to get over that issue.

**Rhythmic swing.** Rhythm is important in golf, and a swing with lag is usually going to have better rhythm and tempo than a swing which releases the club head prematurely. That means that you should be able to make your swing more consistent day in and day out, leading to better scores in the long run.

Many golfers ignore the importance of rhythm in the game, as they focus only on the technical positions that they need to hit instead. Technical positions are important, of course, but they aren't going to get you anywhere unless you have a beautiful rhythm to match.

An impact bag is a great tool that can be used to improve many parts of your game, including your ability to lag the clubhead into the ball. Use the information above to fine-tune your swing technique as it relates to lag, and you could be on the road to hitting the longest and straightest shots of your golfing life.

# CHAPTER 14: <u>SHALLOWER BUNKER</u> <u>SWING</u>

**M**ost golfers know they're supposed to hit behind the ball in a greenside bunker, causing the sand to toss the ball up, out, and onto the green. Many get into trouble, however, by hitting the sand at too steep of an angle.

When you chop down sharply behind the ball, clubhead speed is lost and the ball goes only a short distance – often not far enough to escape the bunker. Instead, the clubhead should enter on a shallower angle and continue through to a normal finish position, rather than staying stuck in the sand.

The common swing fault is to use the arms and wrists exclusively, picking up the club abruptly and smacking straight down. It's important to remember that, just like a shot from grass, you must make an actual golf swing in the bunker.

**If you have a tendency to chop down and come up short, try these tips to improve your bunker play:**

**Stand farther from the ball:** If you're right on top of the ball, your swing will be too upright (vertical). Moving back a few inches will flatten out your swing and the angle of approach.

**Open the clubface:** Often, players will address the ball with the clubface square to the target line or even slightly closed. Instead, set up with the clubface pointing just right of your target in an open position, which will add loft and help you get the ball up.

**Take the club back low:** As you hover the club behind the ball (remember, touching the sand, called "grounding" the club, invokes a two-stroke penalty), focus on keeping it close to the surface on the backswing. This will shallow out your motion and the clubhead's path.

**Turn your body through the shot:** Probably the No. 1 fundamental golfers forget on bunker shots is that your body must turn all the way through to the finish. Choose the spot behind the ball you want to hit – about 2 inches is standard – then swing through the spot, not into it. Finish with your chest facing the target and your arms in front of your body.

Here's an easy reminder: Digging is for the beach. Proper bunker play"> is about throwing the sand, not chopping it.

## Improve Sand Shots with Shallower Swing

Playing from the sand is a difficult task for many amateur golfers. One of the biggest challenges that come along with bunker shots is the fact that the technique you use from the sand is dramatically different from the technique you use on the rest of the course.

To be a successful bunker player, you need to spend time specifically learning how to make a swing that can loft your ball up out of the sand time after time. This technique isn't the most complicated thing you will learn on the golf course, but it does need to be learned nonetheless. If you take bunker shots for granted, they will always be a weakness of your game – and they will continue to cost you shots round after round.

In this chapter, we are going to talk about the proper technique to use for hitting sand shots. Specifically, we are going to be addressing greenside sand shots, as those are different from shots hit out of the fairway bunkers.

Greenside bunker shots are an important skill to develop, as you need to be able to blast the ball out close to the hole to set up par-saving putts after you have missed the green. Most courses feature greenside bunkers on nearly every hole, meaning this is a shot that you are going to have to call on frequently.

Even the best players in the game miss greens from time to time, so playing from the sand is inevitable. Take some time to hone this part of your golf game and the rewards will soon show themselves on the scorecard.

One of the best ways to improve on your sand shot technique is to shallow out the path of your swing. Countless amateur players swing down into the ball on a path that is too steep – a mistake that causes a number of problems. A steep downswing when hitting a greenside bunker shot is going to cause the ball to come out low, it is going to make it difficult to judge the distance of your shot, and it is going to limit the amount of backspin you put on the ball.

All of these issues can be solved simply by shallowing out the swing slightly as you move through the sand. A shallow path is a preferred approach by nearly every professional golfer, and you should be following that lead.

Before getting into the details of the proper technique for a greenside bunker shot, it should be stated that you are going to need to practice your technique regularly if you are going to have success. Greenside bunker shots require not only good technique but also plenty of 'feel' in order to be hit properly.

If you lack that feel, which can only be developed in practice, you will struggle to hit the ball the right distance – even if your technique is picture-perfect. Carve out at least a few minutes during each practice session to spend in a practice bunker and you will be well on your way to improved results from the sand.

All of the content below is based on a right-handed golfer. If you happen to play left-handed, please take a moment to reverse the directions as necessary.

## Understanding Greenside Sand Shots

It would be fair to say that greenside bunker shots are almost completely opposite from any other shot you hit on the course. All of the fundamentals that you learn throughout the rest of the game – with the exception of keeping your head down – are going to go out the window when in a greenside bunker. For these kinds of short sand shots, you will need to learn a completely new technique that you can use in just this specific situation.

To get a clear overall picture of what you are going to be trying to accomplish while down in a greenside bunker, check out the following points –

**You aren't actually going to hit the ball.** That's right – when you execute a greenside bunker shot swing correctly, you are going to miss the golf ball. The wedge you are using will slide right under the ball, and it will be the momentum of the sand between your club and the ball that carries the ball up and out of the hazard.

This is a difficult concept for most amateurs to grasp at first, and it is why many players struggle with bunker shots for a long period of time. On the rest of the course, your number one objective is to hit the ball cleanly, but that changes in the sand. Work on moving your club under the ball cleanly and trust the sand to do its job in carrying the ball out and onto the green.

**You will need to swing hard.** This is another one of the tricky points that come along with playing from the sand. Even though most of your sand shots will be played from within just a few yards of the putting surface, you will still need to swing quite hard on the average bunker shot. The resistance that is provided by the sand will dramatically slow your club down through the hitting area, meaning you are going to need to enter the sand with plenty of force in order to come out on the other side.

Also, since you aren't hitting the ball directly, very little of the power from your swing is actually going to be passed on to the ball itself. This is one of the many reasons why practice is so important when it comes to bunker play.

With practice, you will get comfortable with the kind of swing you need to make in order to splash the ball out cleanly onto the green.

**You will need to read the sand.** Sand conditions can vary wildly from course to course, and even from day to day on the same course. When you play a shot from a bunker with the firm, hard-packed sand, the ball is going to come out quickly and you will need less swing speed to play the shot.

On the other hand, dry and fluffy sand is going to soak up a lot of the energy of your swing, meaning you will have to swing quite hard to reach the target. Also, shots played from firm sand tend to spin more than those played from soft sand, so that is yet another variable to keep in mind. As you gain experience, you will get more and more comfortable with the task of reading your lie in greenside bunkers.

**You will need to dig in.** One of the basic fundamentals of good greenside bunker play is a simple move that you will make with your feet prior to the swing. As you take your stance, be sure to wiggle both of your feet from side to side in order to set them down into the sand nicely. This move will give you stable footing for the swing to come.

The four points above should give you a good indication of the idea behind playing a greenside bunker shot. Below, we will get into more specific detail on the way you are going to swing your wedge on the typical greenside explosion shot.

## Building a Good Stance

Before you make any swing in a bunker – or anywhere else on the course, for that matter – you need to build a good stance. We already touched on one of the points that you need to hit in your stance (wiggling your feet into the sand), but there are other fundamentals to watch for as well. Hit on the points listed below and you can be sure that your stance is going to promote a quality swing as you play from the sand.

**Deep flex in your knees.** You should have more flex in your knees when playing a greenside bunker shot than you would when making a full swing anywhere else on the course. Why? It comes down to the way the club needs to move through the sand.

Since you need to actually swing the club under the ball, you are going to want to lower the overall level of your body at address – and the best way to do that is through knee flex. Keep your back straight and your chin up while addressing the ball with plenty of bend in your knees and you will be in the perfect position for quality bunker shots.

**Forward ball position.** If you are going to swing through your bunker shots on a shallow path, you are going to need to play these shots from a forward ball position. While the exact positioning of the ball should depend on the length of the shot at hand and the lie that you have in the sand, you should at least be playing the ball slightly forward of center.

Moving the ball back in your stance will automatically cause your swing to be steeper, so avoid that ball position unless you have a terrible lie in the sand.

**Open to the target line.** Another one of the key fundamentals for a greenside bunker shot is cutting across the ball at impact. You want to be swinging from outside-in through the hitting area, as this type of path will allow you to add both height and backspin to your shots. To make it as easy as possible to swing across the line, consider opening up your stance at address.

When you want to hit a high and short bunker shot, it will be necessary to open your stance dramatically. Or, if you want to drive the ball lower to a target that is on the other side of the green, you can bring your stance back close to a square position.

**Chin up.** This is one of those rare points that apply both in the bunker and throughout the rest of the course. When taking your stance over a greenside bunker shot, be sure to keep your chin up and away from your chest.

This is important because you are going to need a big shoulder turn in order to generate the kind of speed necessary to carve the ball out of the bunker. If you were to play the shot with your chin down, your shoulder turn would be restricted and your swing would lack the speed it needs to be successful.

**Lay the face open.** Perhaps the most important single key for your setup in a greenside bunker is opening up the face of your wedge dramatically at address. Even though you are likely using a wedge with around 55 degrees of loft, you should still open the face further – to the point where it is almost pointed directly up at the sky.

Adding loft will not only help the ball get up into the air quickly, but it will also expose the bounce on the sole of the club to the sand. That bounce is going to help the wedge glide through the sand, which may not happen if you chose to keep the face square to the target line.

The stance you use when playing from a bunker is going to say a lot about the quality of the shots you are able to produce.

## Playing the Shot Properly

Setting up properly over the ball is a big part of the job, but you still have work to do before you can find your ball resting within a few feet of the cup. After completing your setup, you need to have a clear picture of the kind of swing you are going to make. First, you are going to need to be patient as you allow this swing to develop naturally from start to finish.

You can't rush your bunker shots, as you have to give the swing the time it needs to generate speed. If you cut your backswing short while in a hurry to hit the shot, you will struggle to produce the necessary power and the ball might not get out of the bunker at all. Rhythm and tempo are important fundamentals throughout the game of golf, and that certainly applies when playing from the sand.

In addition to giving your swing plenty of time to develop, you also need to make a great shoulder turn going back. This is a point that was touched on previously, but it needs to be highlighted again due to its importance. As the swing goes back, you want to do your best to turn your back to the target by the time you reach the top of the swing.

If you are only swinging back with your arms, it will be hard to develop the necessary power, and you also won't have as much control over the path of the swing coming back down. During the backswing, think about moving your left shoulder under your chin by the time you reach the top – if you manage that point, you will have done well with your turn.

As the backswing finishes and the downswing begins, we start to see where the concept of a shallow path through the ball really comes into play. During the downswing, you should be using your right hand aggressively to fire the clubhead under the ball.

This is something that you would never want to do when making a swing from the grass, but it is exactly the right move to make in the sand. With your right hand taking over the downswing, the club will be quickly accelerating and you should be able to slip the wedge under the ball with no trouble at all.

Many amateur golfers struggle with this point because they have learned to keep their right hand out of the action on all of their other swings. By practicing this important key, however, you can learn how to employ the use of your right hand while playing sand shots.

The final key that you need to keep in mind with regard to your greenside bunker swing is the fact that you only want to move into an abbreviated follow-through. Rather than a full finish with your right heel off the ground and your hands above your head, you want to cut off the follow-through in order to maintain loft on the club. Hold the face open to the target, cut your finish off at about waist high, and keep your eyes down on the sand until the ball is up and out of the bunker.

## When a Shallow Swing Won't Work

Most of the time, you are going to be well-served by using a shallow swing through the hitting area in a greenside bunker. However, that is not always going to be the case. Sometimes, you are going to have to attack the ball at a steeper angle in order to achieve the desired result. The points below highlight some occasions when you should opt for a steeper swing through the sand.

**A buried lie.** When your golf ball is buried deep down in the sand, you are going to have no choice but to make a steep swing that can gouge the ball out of the bunker. These lies are most likely to occur when you are playing a course with soft sand, but they can also happen when your ball comes down into a bunker from a high trajectory.

You aren't going to have much control over the ball when playing from a buried lie, so your goal should be to simply get the ball out of the bunker and back onto the grass. Even if you aren't able to get onto the putting surface, placing your ball on the grass will is progress and it will let you limit the damage on a given hole.

**A long greenside bunker shot.** Most greenside bunker shots are rather short, but you will face long greenside bunker shots from time to time. If you find yourself facing a greenside bunker shot of 30 yards or more, shift to a steeper swing in order to cover the distance in front of you more easily.

It is hard to hit the ball far enough in this instance with a shallow swing, so give yourself a better chance of success by swinging down steeply into the sand. Of course, you need to have a low bunker lip in front of you in order to use this strategy, as you have to make sure to hit the ball high enough to get out of the sand in the first place.

**Extremely firm/wet sand.** To play an explosion shot with a shallow swing, you need to have at least a few inches of relatively soft sand under the ball. When that is the case, you can proceed as usual with your shallow swing from a forward ball position.

However, if the sand is firm and hard-packed – such as it can be after a rainstorm – you won't be able to take that path. Instead of digging into the sand and under the ball, your wedge will bounce off of the sand and you will likely blade the shot. To avoid that outcome, forget about swinging shallow and instead hit a pitch shot with a steep downswing. You aren't going to blast this shot as usual from the sand, as the conditions simply won't allow it.

Play this shot from the back of your stance, swing down as you would when pitching from the grass, and keep your head perfectly still. You need great nerves to execute this shot, but it can save the day when a regular explosion just won't work.

Bunker shots will always be tricky and a little bit unpredictable, but they can be made far easier with good technique and some practice. Use the information provided throughout this chapter to guide your upcoming practice sessions and your bunker game should improve in short order. With increased confidence from the sand, you should find that you are able to get up and down more frequently, and your scores should come down as a result.

# CHAPTER 15: PITCHING PROBLEMS

S o you have hit a fantastic tee shot straight down the middle of the fairway and you only have 75 yards left on to the green. All you have to do is play a three quarter pitch shot on to the green, ideally close to the flag to make the best possible chance to make a birdie.

Sounds simple, however even the most basic of pitch shots can be a problem for golfers who do not play the shot correctly and most effectively. This then leads to a lack of confidence and errors start to slip in. What used to be a very simple and easy shot has now become many golfer's nightmare shot. This tip is designed to help with your issues and help you overcome your pitching problems.

Fault - Many golfers play the pitch shot with the wrong part of the sole of the golf club, normally using the leading edge to make contact with the ground, therefore digging the leading edge into the turf too much resulting in inconsistent connections and poor strikes. In turn, this poor technique can cause a lack of confidence and flow to the pitching technique.

**Cure -** It is very important to set up the pitch shot in the correct manner to allow the club to strike the ball on a slightly descending blow into the golf ball, without digging into the ground. The main factors to a great set up when pitching is to set up with the aim being to minimize the power created by the body and the golf club to help control the golf shot more effectively.

One area of the golf swing that helps create power is the width of the stance, so make sure you narrow your stance to minimize the amount of power that can be applied. Also, the distance away from the golf ball creates power so stand slightly closer to the golf ball to minimize this power source too. Standing slightly closer helps with a more upright golf swing to help impart a downward blow into the golf ball.

**Key tip** - Apply about 60% of your body weight on to the front side and keep it on the front foot for the duration of the golf shot. This will help with a slight descending strike to promote clean contact.

**Key point** - Use the bounce on your golf wedge to help cleaner strikes. Most modern wedges now have a bounce angle on the bottom of the golf club (bounce is the angle difference between the leading edge and the trailing edge). Bounce angle is used to help the golf club exit the ground once the club has entered the surface.

To use the bounce angle most effectively, we have to feel like the trailing edge of the golf club is making contact with the ground as opposed to the leading edge digging into the floor. When you set up a practice shot, aim to skim the floor with the trailing edge of the sole of the wedge.

You should notice the golf club slides effortlessly across the surface without much friction. This method will really help you to make a cleaner contact when pitching from any surface on the golf course.

## How to Improve Your Golf Pitching Problems

When you head to the local driving range to work on your game, do you take time to practice your pitching? If you are like most amateur golfers, the answer to that question is probably 'no'. Most players don't bother to work on their pitching, as they are too concerned with things like hitting long drives, making short putts, etc.

And, of course, there is nothing wrong with working on those parts of your game. However, you need to have a well-rounded game if you are going to shoot low scores. In order to build that well-rounded game, you will want to spend at least some of your practice time learning how to pitch the ball properly.

Despite the fact that pitching is often ignored during practice sessions, it actually is a skill that is called on quite often on the course. When you miss a green, you may get close enough to hit a simple chip shot – or you might need to hit a pitch. There is no exact definition for what is a chip and what is a pitch, but any shot played from between 10 – 30 yards from the target is usually thought of as a pitch.

Without the right technique available to handle this type of shot, you may find that these are some of the trickiest positions on the course. Rather than playing in fear of leaving your ball in this range, learn how to pitch properly and turn a weakness into a strength.

The best way to think about pitching is to imagine it as a miniature version of your full swing. You are going to use the same basic setup and stance, although everything will be tightened up since you are only making a small move through the ball. In fact, learning how to pitch is a great review for the basics of your full swing, since you are going to be in many of the same positions.

If you are having trouble with your full swing, try hitting some pitch shots to remind yourself to get back to the fundamentals. When you are able to pitch the ball using a small version of your regular swing, you will have more consistency throughout the bag.

In this chapter, we are going to provide you with a variety of advice related to properly pitching the ball. There will be tips on both the physical and mental side of this topic, as you have to think properly when pitching, just as you need to have reliable mechanics. Many amateur golfers have a mental hurdle to get over when it comes to the prospect of pitching the ball – hopefully, the advice which follows in this chapter will help you get over that hurdle.

All of the content below is based on a right-handed golfer. If you happen to play golf left-handed, please take a moment to reverse the directions as necessary.

## Basic Pitching Technique

To start, we are going to lay the groundwork for a solid pitching technique. You should have a clear picture of how to pitch the golf ball before you ever arrive at the practice area, or your time will be wasted.

By having a great understanding of the goal you are working towards, you can put your time to good use. There is more to hitting good pitch shots than just technique, but this is the logical place to start. Once you master the basics, you can move on to other important subjects related to this kind of shot.

The key elements in solid pitching technique are listed below.

**A balanced stance.** Everything in golf should start with a balanced stance. No matter what kind of shot you are trying to hit, putting yourself in a balanced position is going to give you the best possible chance for success. When pitching the ball, you want to stand relatively tall with an upright posture in your upper body.

Make sure your knees are flexed, and keep your chin up away from your chest. Some golfers get sloppy with their stance when pitching, as they don't think the swing is long enough to have to worry about their stance. Obviously, this is a mistake. Your stance is always important, regardless of the length of the shot at hand. Settle into a balanced stance before you put the club in motion and pitching the ball will immediately get easier.

**Hands in front of the ball.** You should have your hands slightly in front of the ball at impact when pitching – which means you should have your hands in front of the ball at address as well. Start with your hands just slightly past the ball and then return them to that position as you swing through the shot. It is important to hit down through impact on pitch shots, and getting your hands past the ball is the only way to do that.

With your hands in front of the ball and the clubhead moving down through impact, you will be able to miss any grass which may be sitting behind the ball – meaning you can achieve a cleaner strike and a better shot overall.

**Watch the ball through impact.** One of the very first golf tips you likely received was to keep your eyes on the ball. While there is more to playing good golf than just watching the ball, this certainly is an important point. When pitching, you might be tempted to look up early to see how you have done.

Of course, by looking up, you will run the risk of ruining your shot. Instead of taking your eyes off the ball, be patient, and watch the top of the ball all the way through impact. Once the ball is gone, you are free to look up to see where it is going. It is harder to be disciplined on this point while on the course than it is in practice, so remind yourself of this key before hitting any on-course pitch shot.

**Play the ball in the middle of your stance.** This is a tip that applies to 'standard' pitch shots played from a clean lie. There will be occasions when it will be necessary to move the ball either forward or back in your stance, and those instances will be addressed later in this chapter.

For now, it is important to understand that you should be playing most of your pitch shots from the middle of your stance. This ball position will allow for a clean hit which imparts plenty of backspin on the ball. No matter what club you happen to be using for your pitch shots, playing from the middle of your stance is usually the right idea.

There is nothing complicated about the technique you need to use when pitching the ball. In fact, if your technique is complicated, you are doing it wrong. This should be a simple move from start to finish, with as few moving parts as possible. Simplicity is going to breed consistency, and consistency is always your friend on the golf course. Review the points above before your next practice session and you should be able to take your pitching performance in the right direction.

# The Right Mindset

Your success or failure in the short game is largely going to come down to the way you think. If you have your mind in the right place prior to hitting short shots, you should be able to succeed more often than not. If you are thinking negatively, however – or if you aren't thinking at all – it will be hard to place the ball close to the target. Learn how to use your mind properly when pitching and the fear that is often associated with these kinds of shots will quickly fade away.

So what should you be thinking about while pitching? Try using the following tips.

**Focus your mind on a specific target.** This is by far the number one mistake made by amateur golfers who struggle with their pitching. When the average golfer stands over the ball to hit a pitch shot, what is he or she aiming at? The hole, of course. There is only one problem with that line of thinking – the hole is not actually your target for the shot. Unless you expect the ball to stop immediately where it lands, you need to be aiming for a spot somewhere short of the hole.

That is your true target for the shot, and that is where you should be focusing your attention. Before you ever walk up to take your stance, you should first work on picking out a landing spot for the pitch. Then, as you settle in to make your swing, keep that landing spot in mind and use it as a point of focus. As long as you hit that spot, the rest should take care of itself.

**Call on your practice experience.** Practicing your short game is not just about drilling your technique. Perhaps more importantly, it is about building up your confidence so you can perform properly on the course. When you find yourself facing a tough pitch shot on the course, think back to a similar pitch shot that you have played in practice.

Calling on the successes you have had in practice will make the challenges you face on the course seem a little less daunting. Of course, if this method is going to work, you have to actually practice your pitching in the first place. Carve out a part of each practice session for pitching practice so you can have plenty of confidence available when the time comes.

**Clear your mind.** One of the problems faced by many amateur golfers is failing to ever actually focus on the task at hand before hitting a shot. This is an innocent mistake that actually stems from nothing more than having fun with your friends. As you walk up the fairway toward your ball near the green, you will probably be chatting about various golf or non-golf related topics with your buddies.

Then, as you prepare to hit your shot, you may fail to shift your mind back into 'golf mode'. In many ways, you will be playing the shot on auto-pilot. As you might imagine, that is not a great way to play this difficult game. Golf requires total focus if you are to be successful, so make sure to restore your focus before moving forward. There is nothing wrong with chatting with your friends or playing partners as you move around the course, but always remember that you need to get back to business before hitting a shot.

**Expect success.** There are really only two ways to go when you get ready to hit a pitch shot – you can either expect to be successful, or you can expect to fail. Unfortunately, most amateur golfers fall into the latter category. They are afraid of these kinds of shots, and they expect them to turn out badly as a result.

Planning on failure is no way to play this game. Not only will such a negative attitude have a harmful effect on the quality of your game, but it will also make your time on the course less enjoyable. There is no reason to think so negatively, so expect to hit a great shot every single time you stand over the ball. It won't always happen, but your positivity will improve your performance as a whole.

It is easy to overlook the importance of the mental side of golf when it comes to the short game. After all, this part of the game seems so simple – you don't have to hit the ball hard, and the mechanics of your technique aren't particularly complicated. However, the mental side of the game is always important, no matter how far you are trying to hit a given shot. Dial-in your mental game and watch your results improve almost immediately.

# Adding Variety to Your Pitching

In baseball, a pitcher needs to have a variety of pitches available in order to get the batters out. While this is a different kind of pitching, the concept is the same. Since you are going to face a number of different situations on the course, you need to know how to produce a few different pitch shots when the moment is right. Adding variety to your pitching game will make it easier to get around various golf courses safely.

The following list includes some of the basic chip shot variations you need to consider.

**High-lofted pitch shot.** When you don't have much green to work with, you will want to take the ball in higher in order to stop it quicker. To play the ball higher through the air, move your ball position up closer to your left foot. Also, open the face of your wedge slightly at address to add loft to the club. From there, make your usual swing, being careful to keep your eyes down on the ball. As long as you make clean contact, you should be able to sweep the ball cleanly off the turf and up into the air.

**Pitch and run.** This next shot is just the opposite of the previous option. When you want to pitch the ball down low to the ground to provide it with plenty of bounce and roll, the adjustments you make will not be surprising. You are going to need to move the ball back in your stance, and you will want to close the clubface slightly. If you aren't comfortable closing the clubface, consider using one less club in order to produce a lower flight. You are going to get a tremendous amount of runout with this play, so be sure to give the ball plenty of room to work.

**Pitch from the deep rough.** Hopefully, this is a shot that you don't need to call on very often. When you do find your ball down in the deep rough, however, you are going to need to know how to get yourself out of trouble as soon as possible. To adjust your pitching technique to deal with this situation, start by opening your stance to the target. Also, open the clubface slightly and choke down on the grip of your wedge.

Basically, you are going to play this shot as an explosion shot out of the sand. You are going to make a big swing, and you are going to attempt to move the club under the ball. If all goes well, the ball will pop up and out of the grass, and it will hopefully land on the green. This shot is never going to be particularly easy, but it can be handled more times than not when you use the right technique.

As you practice your pitching at the local course, work on learning a variety of shots in order to add to your repertoire. You should work on each of the three shots above, but you should work on your own creations, as well. Think outside the box, try different techniques, and see what you can come up with. You never know when you might invent a handy pitch shot which is able to help you knock the ball close to the hole from time to time.

## Pitch Shot Troubleshooting

Even when armed with quality advice, many golfers continue to struggle with the skill of pitching the ball onto the green. If you find that your ability in this area is not progressing as you would like, you may be getting caught up on one of the common pitching problems. Below, we have listed a few common problems, along with potential solutions.

**Hitting the ball thin.** Most often, thin pitch shots are the result of moving your head up and out of the shot prematurely. When you move your head early, your shoulders are likely to lift up as well, and the leading edge may catch the ball rather than the actual face of the club. When this problem plagues your game, focus on keeping your eyes on the ball until impact. This tip sounds simple, but it is the only thing that works.

**Hitting the ball too far.** Many golfers struggle to control their distance on pitch shots. If you hit the ball cleanly, it is easy to send it beyond the target when only starting from 20 or 30 yards away. To avoid hitting the ball too far, choke down on the club for control and do your best to focus on a specific landing spot. Distance control is the key to good short gameplay, so spend plenty of time working on your skill in this area.

**Chunking pitch shots.** For many golfers, this is their big fear when they stand over a pitch shot. They are afraid that they will catch the ground prior to the ball, moving the shot only a few feet in front of them in the end. Obviously, this is one of the worst possible outcomes for the shot, so it should be avoided at all costs.

To make sure you don't hit the ball fat, resist the temptation to help the ball up into the air. Most golfers hit fat shots because they are trying to lift the ball – when in reality, the ball does not need to be lifted. The wedge you are holding has plenty of loft to get the ball up into the air all on its own. Hit down through the shot and watch the ball sail easily toward the target.

Pitching is an area of the game which is often overlooked, but that shouldn't be the case much longer for you. If you are willing to focus on this important skill, you can improve your performance around the greens in short order. With improved pitching now a reality, your scores will quickly trend in the right direction.

◆ ◆ ◆

# CHAPTER 16: <u>MORE SPIN ON SAND SHOTS</u>

D on't you wish you could hit those stop-on-a-dime bunker shots like the pros? Maybe you can. It does, however, require an aggressive mentality that many golfers can't seem to summon when their ball is in the sand.

To generate spin, you've got to make an accelerating swing and hit the sand fairly close to the ball. That can be a frightening prospect, conjuring visions of skulled shots that whiz past the heads of your playing partners and end up who knows where.

Fear, of course, is the enemy of great bunker play. It fosters a tentative, please-just-let-me-get-this-out swing that fails to deliver the speed needed for spin.

If you have no trouble escaping the sand but want to improve your results – e.g. get the ball closer – it's time to adopt the pros' mindset. When a pro enters a bunker, he sees no danger but an opportunity. He knows he can spin and control a shot from sand much better than he can from thick rough.

Do keep in mind that all lies aren't created equal. If the sand is extra-soft, your ball is buried or nestled down, you won't be able to impart much spin. It takes a clean lie, preferably from reasonably firm sand, to hit a high-spin blast.

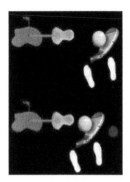

**Here's how it's done:**

1. Set up with your feet and clubface more open than normal. Remember to set the clubface open, then grip the club.

2. Play the ball slightly forward of the middle of your stance.

3. Choose a spot roughly 1-1.5" behind the ball; this is where you want the club to enter.

4. Pick up the club abruptly with your hands and wrists.

5. Accelerate the clubhead into your spot and keep the clubface open on the follow-through, with your left knuckles pointing up.

A good drill is to draw a line in the sand, about 2" wide, and practice hitting the target side of the line. Do this until you can repeatedly hit the spot, then place a ball on the target edge of the line and try it. Make sure there are no golfers (or windows) on the opposite side of the green as you may well blade a few before getting the hang of it.

## *Increase Swing Speed for More Spin on Sand Shots*

Watching golf on TV, it is easy to notice that the average professional golfer possesses a wide range of skills. Simply hitting the ball an impressive distance is not nearly enough to make it to the top of the game.

Pro golfers also need to have control over their ball flights, a solid short game, good decision-making skills, and more. Professional golf is extremely hard, and only those with talent from tee to green are able to survive.

With that in mind, we are going to talk about something in this chapter that professional golfers are able to do with ease – spin their bunker shots. You have certainly seen this time and time again. A pro golfer winds up in a greenside bunker, in what looks to be a difficult position.

With one big swing, however, they loft the ball up out of the trap, land it next to the hole, and the shot stops dead. How did they do that? It looks more like magic than anything else. Amazingly, these kinds of shots are commonplace on the PGA Tour. The type of bunker shot which will scare a typical amateur golfer is simply no problem at all for a top pro.

So how do they do it? That is what we are going to explain in this chapter. By the end of this piece, you should have a clear understanding of how the pros spin their greenside bunker shots, and how you can do the same. Believe it or not, this type of sand shot is actually within the reach of the average player. You might not ever be able to launch a drive 300+ yards down the fairway like your favorite pro, but you can hit beautiful bunker shots with tons of spin.

You won't be surprised to learn that this shot is not going to make its way into your game by accident. Even after reading this chapter and understanding how this shot works, you will still have to spend plenty of time practicing before you can count on the shot to serve you well. Unfortunately, it can be difficult to find a place to practice your bunker shots.

Some golf facilities have a practice bunker you can use in the short game area, but many do not. If your home course does not have such a feature, call around to other area courses to see if you can find somewhere to work on this skill. Nothing in your game will improve without practice, and that certainly applies to this specific kind of bunker shot.

All of the content below is based on a right-handed golfer. If you happen to play left-handed, please take a moment to reverse the directions as necessary.

# Speed and More

First, we are going to talk about what it is that makes a golf ball spin when hit from a greenside bunker. After we have provided you with a clear explanation of this topic, we will then move on to some instruction so you can try this out for yourself. It may take some time to learn how to spin your bunker shots, but the effort will be worth it when you are able to get up and down from some pretty tough spots.

The points listed below will outline exactly what you need to do in order to load up your bunker shots with plenty of spin.

**Use lots of speed.** This is the first part of the equation. As mentioned in the title of this chapter, adding swing speed should help you improve your spin rate – provided you also hit on the other points listed below. Speed alone is not going to cause your shots to spin, but it is a good place to start.

It can be hard to convince yourself that you need to swing hard when you are already close to the target, but that is exactly what needs to happen. Through plenty of practice, you will quickly learn that it is okay to swing hard since the sand is going to take a lot of the power out of your swing at the bottom. In the end, the combination of an aggressive swing and the dampening effect of the sand should lead to a shot that comes out with just the right amount of power.

**Lay the face wide open.** This is another critical part of spinning your sand shots. At address, you should be laying the face wide open so that the club has roughly 80* of loft or more. You will be using a sand wedge with something like 54* - 56* of loft, but the club should be turned much more open than that at address.

For particularly difficult shots where a steep bunker lip is in your way, it might be necessary to lay the face completely open at 90*. Bunker shots need to get up quickly, which is why it is so important to open the face before starting your swing. Also, this setup is going to let the club cut quickly through the sand under the ball, adding the spin you need to stop the ball quickly.

**Take a shallow path.** Many golfers go wrong here. Knowing that they are supposed to plunge the clubhead into the sand in order to send the ball up toward the green, many golfers swing down with a steep angle of attack. That is a mistake, and it will make it impossible to spin the ball. Instead of a steep angle, you should be trying to swing through on a shallow path to take a thin strip of sand out of the bunker. If you can slide your club along the top of the sand while only digging in an inch or so, it will quickly become easier to produce spin.

This is the best way to approach a standard bunker shot, but it isn't going to work effectively when you have a bad lie. If the ball is sitting down in the sand (often called a plugged lie), you will need to make an adjustment and use a steeper swing to gouge the ball out. This kind of shot isn't going to have much spin – or any spin at all – but at least you'll have a chance to get out of the trap.

**Enter the sand close to the ball.** By far, this is the hardest part of the equation. Most golfers know that they need to hit the sand before the ball in order to create a proper explosion shot from a greenside bunker. However, if you take too much sand before the ball, there won't be much spin placed on the shot, and it will take a big bounce and roll after it lands.

You are going to have to move your point of contact with the sand up closer to the ball if you want to really produce some meaningful spin. This, of course, takes a steady nerve. If you make even a small mistake, you could catch too much ball and send the shot flying over the green. Professional golfers are comfortable with this play because they have a high level of skill and plenty of experience. To build up your own confidence, plenty of practice will be required.

As you can see, there are plenty of things that need to come together successfully in order for you to spin the ball when coming out of a bunker. This task is not impossible, so you shouldn't be intimidated by this list. Now that you have the information you need, it is time to get down to work on building the right technique for the shot.

# Build Your Swing

Despite being a shot that takes place within close proximity to the green, this spinning bunker shot has more in common with your full swing than it does with anything in your short game. As mentioned above, you are going to be making a big swing with plenty of speed. If you were to play a shot that resembles your standard chip shot only from the sand, you would have no chance at a great result. Only a big swing will do, which is exactly what we are going to build with the following tips.

**Use a wide stance.** To get started, you are going to set your feet rather far apart in the bunker. This wide stance is going to serve two purposes. First, it will enable you to make an aggressive swing without losing your balance. Also, it is going to promote the shallow angle of attack that you are trying to achieve.

Set your feet just outside of shoulder-width apart for best results. Also, set up with your stance open to the target line that you have picked for the shot. This open stance will let you swing across the ball at impact, which is yet another way to make it easier to spin the ball (and get the ball up in the air quickly).

**Deep flex in your knees.** You will want to flex your knees significantly on this kind of bunker shot. A deep knee flex is going to bring your upper body down closer to the level of the sand, which will help get your club under the ball at impact. Also, the knee flex is another way to flatten your swing path and take a shallow trip through the sand.

While many golfers know to flex their knees at address, it is common for that knee flex to be lost somewhere during the swing. Don't let that happen to you. Focus on maintaining your knee flex throughout the action as you swing back and through.

**Turn your shoulders.** Just as you would when hitting a driver from the tee, you are going to want to make a big shoulder turn on this shot. It is easy to think that you can create enough speed with your hands and wrists alone, but that isn't going to work. Turn your back to the target in the backswing to build up as much potential for speed as possible. Then, unleash all of that speed going forward. This swing is going to be driven by your upper body while your lower body provides a solid base.

**Fire the right hand through the sand.** At the bottom of the swing, this shot becomes all about the right hand. This is where you really add spin to the ball. As the club is entering the sand, fire your right hand aggressively to give the clubhead as much speed as possible. Hopefully, the face of your wedge will rip through the bunker and the ball will come out spinning at a very high rate.

**Finish, finish, finish.** One of the worst things you can do with a bunker shot is given up on the swing before you have made it all the way through to the finish. Quitting on this kind of shot is a sure recipe for failure. Once you have committed to hitting a spinning sand shot with a big swing, you need to simply go for it and don't hold anything back. Swing all the way up into a full finish and trust that the shot is going to come out as expected.

It might seem like there is a lot of information to digest above, but the spinning bunker shot is actually pretty simple when you break it down. Work on one key at a time as you practice, and pretty soon you will have a composed action that is able to produce excellent bunker shots time and again.

## Be Smart

Executing a bunker shot is about both physical techniques and course management decisions. We have already talked about the physical technique you will need to use to send the ball out of the sand with plenty of spin. Now, we are going to move on to the decision making process. Your sand shots need to be carefully planned, just like any other shot you hit.

As you are standing in the sand getting ready to hit this shot, here are the points you want to keep in mind.

**Where will the ball land?** If you are planning to hit a shot with a lot of spin, your landing spot is likely going to be quite close to the hole itself. Even with that in mind, you should take a moment to pick out a specific landing spot before taking your stance and making the swing. Chip and pitch shots are best played when you pick out a landing spot, and the same concept applies in the bunker.

**Are there any major risks?** It is easy to get caught up in trying to hit the ball close to the hole, but sometimes you need to be smart and just make sure you keep the ball out of trouble. Are there any notable issues with this shot that you need to address? For instance, if there is a particularly high lip in front of your ball, or if you don't have a great lie, you will need to think about those concerns before making a swing.

**Can you use a slope?** One of the nice things about spinning a bunker shot is the fact that you can use slopes on or around the greens to help you get the ball closer to the hole. For instance, if you are short-sided to the hole – but there is a slope just beyond the hole which will bring the ball back – you could land the ball on that slope and use the combination of the slope and your spin to bring the ball back toward you. This is something that looks quite impressive when done correctly, so you are sure to impress your playing partners.

**How are the conditions?** If the ground is wet during your round, the spin you place on the ball is not going to have as much of an effect when the ball lands. The water on the greens will cause the stopping power of the backspin to be reduced, meaning the shot is more likely to skid than stop. This issue will be minimal if there is only a light dew on the ground, but it will be a much bigger factor when playing in the rain.

**Is spin the right choice?** On longer bunker shots, it may be better to keep the spin off your ball and simply let the shot bounce and roll toward the hole. Carrying the shot a significant distance before stopping it cold is an extremely difficult task. Leave your spinning bunker shots to the shorter scenarios and take the spin off the ball when playing all the way across the green. To use less spin, simply hit slightly farther behind the ball, and use a slightly steeper swing.

Your newfound ability to hit spinning bunker shots is only going to pay off if you make smart decisions along the way. Of course, that is true of any shot that you learn in this game. Having the ability to play a variety of shots is great, but it isn't going to turn into lower scores without the ability to pick and choose your spots correctly. Think through each shot and consider all options before you make a swing and send the ball on its way.

## Using the Right Golf Ball

If you don't have the right golf balls in your bag, it isn't going to matter how well you execute the technique we have described – you still aren't going to be able to spin your shots effectively. The golf ball you use is by far the biggest factor in whether or not your shots are going to spin. You don't have to use the most expensive ball on the market, but you do have to use a ball that is at least capable of spinning at a high rate when struck correctly.

Fortunately, there is an easy way to judge the ability of a golf ball to spin – just check the price tag. With very few exceptions, you can determine how much spin a ball is capable of holding just by looking at how much it costs.

If you are currently playing with golf balls you picked up out of the discount bin for less than a dollar a ball, you can forget about producing much spin. Those types of golf balls are rock hard, and their firm covers don't allow the club to 'bite' into the ball enough to create backspin. Discount golf balls are great for beginners who are just learning the ropes, but you'll need to upgrade if you want to play shots with spin.

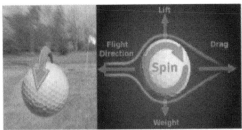

For the average golfer – someone who usually shoots scores between 80 – 95 – the best golf balls are going to be those which cost somewhere between $20 and $30 per dozen. At this level, you will have a ball that is capable of spinning a modest amount around the greens, but it won't spin so much that it is hard to control from the tee.

There is no need for this kind of player to invest in a $40+ per dozen premium ball, as a mid-handicap player simply doesn't have the skills to use such a ball effectively. Unless you are a low-handicapper, stay in the mid-range for golf balls and you will be in good shape.

Hitting a spinning bunker shot from a greenside trap might seem like a high-level skill, but most golfers are capable of pulling this off with the right technique and lots of practice. We hope that the instruction in this chapter will help you add this valuable shot to your repertoire in the near future.

Even if you only pull out the spinning bunker shot once per round, that one shot could set you up for a key up-and-down save. Golf is all about having options and knowing how to get out of as many situations as possible. The spinning bunker shot is one more option you can put in your bag to use at just the right moment.

# CHAPTER 17: <u>INSIDE APPROACH</u>

H ere's a simple truth: If you want to become a good golfer, you must learn to swing the club on an inside-to-outside path.

The inside-out path is preferable to the outside-in swing, or even a clubhead traveling directly down the target line at impact. Among other reasons, an inside-out path is nearly slice-proof, enables you to hit a draw, and transfers more energy to the ball, boosting your power.

Virtually every pro golfer and most low-handicap amateurs swing this way. That includes golfers who favor hitting a fade, such as Jack Nicklaus.

The vast majority of golfers, on the other hand, swing outside-to-in, aka over-the-top. That's usually because they either overuse the arms in relation to the body or fail to transfer weight properly on the backswing and downswing.

It takes time, effort, and a basic understanding of swing mechanics to master the inside-out swing – but if you aim to achieve a single-digit handicap and play consistently solid golf, it's a necessary investment.

## *Why and How to Deliver the Golf Club from Inside the Target Line*

The path that the golf club takes into the ball is extremely important when it comes to determining the final destination of the shot. Countless golfers struggle with a poor swing path, and they pay the price in the form of off-target results. Of course, the most common mistake in the amateur game is the slice, which is usually the result of a swing that comes into the ball from outside-in. Countless golfers deal with a slice for their entire life on the course, simply because they are unable to correct their errant swing path.

In this chapter, we are going to talk about swinging the club in the opposite direction. Instead of coming across the ball through the hitting area, we are going to suggest that you swing from the inside-out. There are many benefits to this method, which we will touch on later in the chapter. Once you learn how to swing from the inside-out properly, you will be surprised to find just how powerful and consistent your game can become.

It should be noted right away that this is one of the most difficult changes you can make to your game. If you are comfortable with swinging across the ball from outside-in at the moment, it is going to be rather strange to approach the ball from the other direction. Making this change successfully is going to require plenty of hard work and patience.

There will be struggles along the way, and your game might even get worse before it gets better. To succeed, you'll need to focus on the long term benefits and be willing to sacrifice the state of your game in the short term. In the end, however, you will be glad you stuck it out when you are able to hit the best shots of your life.

All of the content in this chapter is written from the perspective of a right-handed golfer. If you happen to play left-handed, please take a moment to reverse the directions as necessary.

## The Benefits of an Inside-Out Delivery

As mentioned above, it is going to take some time to learn this move, especially if you have a significantly outside-in path at the moment. So why would you go through all of the hard work and frustration required to make this change? That is what we are going to discuss in this section.

We feel that it is best to provide you with some motivation upfront before you get started with this process. Then, when the going gets tough and you are struggling to find your way on the practice range, you can remember these benefits and stick it out until you reach your goals.

The following points highlight the key benefits of swinging the club through the ball on an inside-out path.

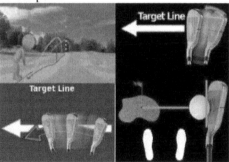

**Added power.** This is the main reason golfers are persuaded to make the switch to an inside-out swing path. When you deliver the club on this path, you should be able to both create more power and transfer more of that power into the golf ball. When you swing down from the outside, you are forced to use mostly your arms and your hands to propel the club through the hitting area. This is not a recipe for power.

On the other hand, a swing that moves from inside-out is able to use body rotation more effectively, forcing the club through the ball with authority. As soon as you are able to adjust your path and successfully swing from inside-out, you will likely notice a significant difference in the way your shots feel coming off the club. When you strike the ball just right after coming down on an inside path, there are few feelings better in the world of golf.

**Controlling your trajectory.** We already mentioned that the slice is a common outcome when swinging across the ball from outside-in. However, even if you don't hit a slice with your current swing path, you might not have as much control over your trajectory as you would like. Swings that move across the ball on an outside-in path tend to create a high rate of backspin, which is not always a good thing.

Plenty of backspin is fine on short iron shots, but it can make your longer shots very difficult to control. Using an inside-out path is going to flatten your angle of attack through the ball, letting you hit a neutral shot that is easier to keep on target. You can still use other methods to hit the ball higher when you would like, and you can even bring the ball down lower more easily when the situation calls for such a shot. Playing good golf is all about controlling your ball as you move around the course. Using an inside-out path is going to make it much easier to do just that.

**Add variety to your game.** When you swing from outside-in, your options are limited in terms of the shot shapes you can create. You will naturally hit a fade/slice, and that is the pattern you'll see on most of your shots. Also, you could hit a pull if you use your hands actively to close down the face at impact. For most players, that will be just about it.

Those are really the only shots you will see consistently leaving your clubface when you swing from outside the line. The story is quite different when you swing from inside-out. You should have little trouble hitting a draw from this position, of course, as swinging out through the ball is the perfect way to impart draw-spin. What you might not know, however, is that you can still hit a fade with this type of swing. In fact, this just might be the best way to create a controlled, powerful fade.

If you swing through on an inside-out path with the clubface slightly open in relation to the swing path, a fade will be the result. Most of the time, when you see a professional golfer hit a fade, this is the way it was created. It will take time and practice, but you can learn how to hit fades and draws on command when you play with an inside-out path.

Once you gain an understanding of the importance of this type of swing path, you will be easily convinced that this is the best thing for your game. It might not be easy to learn how to swing from inside-out, but clearing this hurdle and mastering this move is one of the best things you can do for the improvement of your play. The vast majority of quality golfers are able to swing along this path, and you should strongly consider doing the same.

## Getting Started

With a challenge this significant, it is hard to know where to get started. Fortunately, there is a place you can start which will help to set you up for success as you move along – your address position. By working on your address position right at the start of this process, you can check it off as a point of concern. It is hard enough to hit good golf shots when you have a great stance working for you – without a good stance, you have almost no chance.

So what is it about your address position that will help you swing along an inside-out path? Check out the following tips for help.

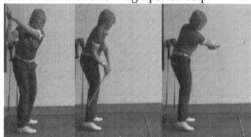

**As square as possible.** Before you walk up to take your stance, you should have picked out a target line for the shot at hand. That imaginary line is going to serve as your point of reference when you create your stance. Everything that makes up your stance should be as square as possible to that chosen target line.

That means your feet, knees, hips, and shoulders should all be equidistant from the line you are using for the shot. Building a perfectly square stance is a great way to leave all of your options open during the swing. Unfortunately, many golfers set up in a way that naturally promotes an outside-in swing.

Many amateurs start with their hips and shoulders open to the line, which leads to a takeaway that moves outside the target line. It should be no surprise that these kinds of swings often come back down on that same path, and a slice is the result. If necessary, use a mirror or video recording equipment to check on your stance and make sure you are finding a square position before moving on.

**Healthy knee flex.** Another common mistake seen among golfers who hit a slice is using very little knee flex at address. During the golf swing – especially during the downswing – your lower body has a critical role to play.

If you fail to flex your knees properly, your legs won't be able to get involved in the action and your swing will be mostly arms and hands. That is bad news, as your arms and hands are almost certainly going to force the club outside the target line on the way down.

Without a good lower body turn, your body will actually be in the way of the club if it wanted to take an inside-out path. With that option off the table, the club is going to find its way down to the ball by moving outside and cutting across at impact. Start with your knees flexed and it will be much easier to keep your legs engaged all the way through the swing.

**Relaxed arm hang.** The takeaway phase of the golf swing is an extremely important, and often-overlooked part of your technique. We will talk about the takeaway more in the next section, but rest assured that this piece of the puzzle has a prominent role to play. To give yourself the best possible chance at making a clean takeaway, you will want to start with a relaxed arm hang at address.

Your arms should be hanging freely from your shoulders, without reaching out or being stuck in close to your body. When viewed from behind, it should be easy to see that your arms are hanging pretty close to vertically. If you are too far off this mark, it will be tough to hit good shots.

To be honest, a solid address position is important for just about every element of your game. Not only is this going to help you swing the club on an inside-out path, but it is simply going to help you play better golf all the way around. Most golfers don't find this to be a particularly exciting element to practice, but you would be wise to work through it for the betterment of your game.

# CHAPTER 18: <u>FOOTING ON LOOSE</u> <u>GROUND</u>

T oday's golf courses often feature vast "waste areas," which are basically sand bunkers that are seldom if ever raked. Many waste areas are extremely firm, with a thin layer of sand on top. You may also encounter pine straw, patches of loose soil, and other places where footing is less than sure.

When they find the ball in such a spot, many golfers focus on the lie -- whether the ball is sitting down, if there are clumps of sand or turf behind it, and so forth. But the key to playing from the unstable ground is to remain steady over the shot.

**Here's how:**

Take one or two more clubs than the yardage calls for. (If it's normally an 8-iron, choose a 6- or 7-iron instead).

Stand with your feet spaced shoulder-width apart – the insides of your feet directly below the outsides of your shoulders.

If possible, dig your feet just into the surface for extra stability, kicking away pebbles or other loose impediments underfoot.

Flex your knees for added balance.

Grip down on the club and play the

ball about mid-stance.

Make a smooth, slightly abbreviated swing, with a shorter finish than usual.

The widened stance, knee flex, and short swing will help you keep your balance and prevent the feet from slipping, ensuring better contact.

Footwork is something that is easy to overlook in golf.

With so much else to think about in your swing – your grip, your shoulder turn, your head position, and on and on – it is easy to forget about your feet. And, most of the time, this is fine. Your feet shouldn't need much help to do their job on a regular swing, as they should remain mostly quiet while helping to keep your steady and balanced from start to finish.

This all changes, however, when you have to stand on loose ground. On certain parts of the course, you may not have the kind of secure footing that you typically enjoy on the tee or in the middle of the fairway. When your footing is questionable, suddenly everything about your swing will feel uncertain. Even a minor slip during the swing can lead to an ugly outcome, so you do need to know how to handle this situation when it comes up.

In this chapter, we are going to provide you with advice on how to deal with the loose ground on the golf course. You certainly don't have to give up on the idea of hitting a good shot just because your footing is dicey, but you will need to make some changes to your approach.

Playing good golf is all about adapting to the circumstances you find on each shot, and that concept is perfectly illustrated here. As soon as you notice that you'll be standing on loose footing, you will need to quickly decide how you are going to handle the shot in order to achieve a successful outcome.

All of the content below is written from the perspective of a right-handed golfer. If you happen to play left-handed, please take a moment to reverse the directions as necessary.

## Common Types of Loose Ground

The type of loose ground you are likely to encounter on the golf course is going to depend greatly on where you play your golf. The surrounding environment and climate is going to determine the types of surfaces you can find when you stray from the fairway. With that said, nearly every environment is going to present some kind of uncomfortable spot from where you may have to hit a shot from time to time.

Let's take a look at some common examples of loose ground that you may encounter on the golf course.

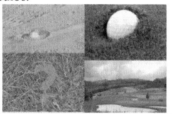

**Bunkers.** This is the obvious one, as nearly every golf course you will ever play will include at least a few sand bunkers. It's usually pretty easy to keep your footing in a greenside bunker, but it can get trickier as you are forced to make longer and longer swings.

The condition of the sand is going to have a big impact on your footing, so always check on this point when getting ready to hit your shot. Generally speaking, it is dry and soft sand which is going to give you trouble from a footing perspective. In bunkers where the sand is damp and hard packed, it should be easier to keep your feet under control.

**Pine straw.** If you play golf in an area where pine straw collects on the ground during a certain time of the year, you'll need to pay careful attention when your ball ends up among the straw. Swinging on pine straw can be extremely slippery in the right circumstances, so it may be tough to make your normal swing without losing balance.

**Waste areas.** These are areas off to the side of the fairways and rough, where the ground has just been left in its natural state. For some courses, that means it will be a desert landscape, with nothing more than sand and maybe a few bushes. The exact makeup of the waste area will depend on the environment surrounding the course.

No matter what it looks like, however, you should expect that your footing will not quite be what it is when on the grass. After all, golf shoes are meant for use on grass, so they are designed specifically to keep your feet in place on the turf. When you stray from the turf, you can't necessarily expect your shoes to perform as they would otherwise.

**Long grass.** In some cases, you may have your feet slip out from under you during a swing when playing from long grass. This isn't 'loose ground' necessarily, but it is still a situation where you need to pay attention to your footing.

Particularly long rough can get matted down under your feet when you take a stance, and that means that your golf shoes may not be able to bite into the turf as they would when on shorter grass. You should pay specific attention to this concern when hitting from a sidehill lie since your weight will not be directly centered over your feet during the swing.

**Wet grass.** The last point on our list is another one which isn't technically loose ground, but it can still give you trouble. When the ground is wet from a recent – or ongoing – rain, you might find that it's difficult to keep your footing during the swing.

This is particularly true if you wear golf shoes that don't have a lot of grip built into the soles, or if your shoes are old and have worn down significantly. If you regularly play golf in the rain, or if you play in an environment where the ground is often wet, you'll need to be very familiar with how to make a swing on wet grass without slipping.

In days gone by, golfers didn't have to worry much about footing thanks to their metal spikes. When playing golf in shoes with metal spikes, it was very difficult to slip during the swing. Of course, metal spikes are long gone, and slipping has become a bit more of an issue. You can still get a great grip on the turf in modern golf shoes, but that grip might not translate quite as well when you leave the grass.

So, why don't golfers still use metal spikes? Well, for one thing, most courses have rules against them now. And for good reason – metal spikes are hard on golf courses, especially greens. The move away from metal has been a great thing for the game overall, as golf courses tend to be in much better condition now than they were years ago.

The rest of this chapter will be dedicated to helping you maintain your footing when the ground is loose. While it is a good idea to prepare yourself to playoff loose ground, what's even better is to keep your ball out of these situations in the first place. By staying on the short grass as often as you can, you'll be able to forget about the loose ground that may be waiting off to the sides of the course.

## Three Basic Adjustments

As you make your way around the golf course during a round, you want to keep your adjustments as minimal as possible. If you are constantly trying to change your swing in significant and dramatic ways, you are just asking for trouble. It's hard enough to find consistency on the course when using the same swing – it's nearly impossible when you alter your technique at every turn.

With that said, you do have to adapt to this game if you want to play up to your potential. Golf is such a fun game in large part because it presents you with an endless list of challenges. You never know exactly what you are going to find when you head out onto the course, even if you have played that course hundreds of times before. The best golfers are those who can adapt on the fly, tailoring their game to the situation at hand.

So, where does that leave us? Basically, you should know that it will be necessary to make adjustments on the course, but you should keep those adjustments as minimal as possible. Toward that end, we have listed three adjustments below that you can use when playing from loose ground. None of these three are going to dramatically change your swing, but they will alter it in a way that helps you keep your footing.

**Narrow your stance.** At first, you might be a bit surprised – and even confused – by this suggestion. Most of the time, when you want to solidify your stance and give yourself a strong base on which to swing, you will widen your stance. That is not the case when you are on loose ground, however. You want to keep your feet directly under your body, so they have as much weight pushing down on them as possible.

When you move your feet out to the sides, you'll actually be more likely to slip. This is especially true during the transition from backswing to downswing. With a wide stance, it is very possible that your right foot will slip out from under you as the swing changes directions. By bringing your stance in and placing your feet roughly below your shoulders, you should find it easier to stay in control.

**Shorten your backswing.** This is a point that really works in tandem with the first point. In addition to narrowing your stance, you also want to shorten up your backswing. This will help you stay over the ball, remain balanced, and avoid the dreaded slip that can occur when trying to make a hard swing.

You are in a tricky spot when you venture onto loose ground, so you shouldn't expect too much from your swing. Instead of going all out, make a controlled swing, and use plenty of club so you can reach the target with relative ease. Save your aggressive swings for shots from the tee or the fairway, when you have good footing and a sizable target.

**Choke down on the grip of the club.** The last adjustment we are going to suggest simply has you gripping down slightly on the handle of the club. By moving your hands down away from the top of the grip, you'll gain some control and make it easier to achieve solid contact.

This is important, as most of the situations which leave you with loose footing also cause you to have a questionable lie. In addition, choking down is naturally going to lead you to a shorter swing, which was the second point we highlighted in this list. You don't have to choke down dramatically to see a benefit – even coming down an inch or two should do the job.

It should be clear that none of the points above represents a dramatic change from your usual swing technique. In fact, you are going to be changing anything at all about the shape or style of your swing. You are simply going to make a couple of pre-swing adjustments – moving your feet closer together and choking down on the grip – and you are going to tighten up your backswing as well.

That's it. It's simple, but it should be quite effective when you do find yourself standing on loose ground.

# CHAPTER 19: FLYER LIE

R ough that borders fairways is generally meant to punish golfers by making it harder to advance the ball all the way to the green. But sometimes, rough has the opposite effect – and that can cause even bigger headaches.

The so-called "flyer lie" usually occurs in lighter rough that offers little or no resistance to the clubhead. Instead, the grass is just fluffy enough to come between the ball and clubface, preventing the grooves from grabbing the ball and imparting backspin.

The result: A knuckling shot that flies farther than planned, then takes off running when it lands. Since many greens drop off sharply to the back -- often into trees or other trouble -- going long is often much worse than falling short.

So how do you know if you're dealing with a flyer? Look for grass behind your ball that's long enough to interfere with the clubface, but not so thick that it will slow the club down. Grass growing toward your target – rather than away from it – is another sure sign you're in flyer-ville.

Southern Bermuda grass is notorious for producing flyers, especially when it's dry. "Stickier" grasses, like bent, rye, and fescue are less flyer-prone. Grass that's heavy with moisture tends to slow the club – reducing flyers – while dew or light rain increases the risk of flyers.

**Here are a few basic steps for dealing with flyer lies:**

**Take less club:** If your distance calls for, say, a 7-iron, hit an 8-iron or even a 9, depending on whether you're better off missing short or long.

**Aim short of the green:** If you're playing to a green that's open in front, choose the club that will land the ball short. Its lack of spin will send the ball bouncing onto the green.

**Play the ball farther back in your stance:** Let's say you've picked a 7-iron, which you normally play in the middle of your stance. Move it an inch or so toward your right foot (for right-handers) to create a steeper swing and minimize clubface contact with grass.

**One more thing:** A ball that's found the fairway isn't necessarily immune. In fact, lightly wet fairways are a key flyer breeding ground, since water fills the grooves on contact. That's one reason professional caddies are obsessive about keeping clubs dry. No one wants to get fired over a flyer.

## Keys to Handling the Flyer Lie

The flyer lie is one of the trickiest situations in golf. When you 'catch a flyer', the ball is likely to shoot over your target and not come to rest until it has found some kind of trouble. As a beginning golfer, you probably thought of shots out of the rough as ones which would land short of the green.

That is usually true, but as you learn as you gain experience, sometimes shots from the rough just don't want to come down at all. These flyers can be seriously damaging to your scorecard, so you need to know how to handle them as effectively as possible.

In this chapter, we are going to cover this topic from all angles. We will define what a flyer lie is and how you can recognize it before hitting your shot. Also, we will discuss the adjustments you can make to reduce the chances of actually hitting a flyer.

This shot will always be a possibility when playing from the rough, but you can improve your odds of avoiding it by taking the right steps. The flyer is even a possibility in the short game, so we are going to talk about that area of play as well.

So what is a flyer? Basically, this is a shot that is hit from the rough and comes out with very little spin. Without the backspin necessary to climb up into the sky, the ball will hold a flat trajectory and carry for a surprising distance. Then, when it lands, it will usually take a couple of big bounces, again due to the lack of backspin.

The golfer has very little control over the ultimate destination of the shot when a flyer occurs. Once you feel that a flyer has taken place, all you can do is ask the ball to get down and hope for the best.

This is different from a 'normal' shot out of the rough because of the velocity involved. Regular shots out of the rough don't have much spin either, but they don't have the speed of a flyer. The rough around the ball slows down the club so much that the shot comes out short and lacking spin.

When you watch a golf tournament on TV where there is deep rough in play, these are usually the kinds of shots you see. However, most golf courses that are open to the public don't keep long rough, so flyers are extremely common. In fact, when you drive the ball into the rough, you should probably be more worried about hitting a flyer than anything else.

All of the content below is written from the perspective of a right-handed golfer. If you happen to play left-handed, please take a moment to reverse the directions as necessary.

# How to Spot a Flyer Lie

If you are going to handle a flyer lie successfully, you first have to see it coming. While you are never going to be able to predict this type of shot with 100% accuracy, you can watch for signs that will make a flyer more likely.

As with anything else in golf, experience is going to play a big role here. The more golf you play, and the more times you find your ball in the rough, the better you will get and deciding what is and isn't a flyer lie.

To help jump-start your education on this point, please review the following tips.

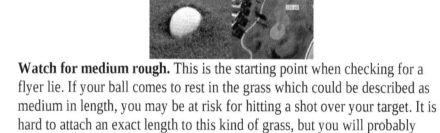

**Watch for medium rough.** This is the starting point when checking for a flyer lie. If your ball comes to rest in the grass which could be described as medium in length, you may be at risk for hitting a shot over your target. It is hard to attach an exact length to this kind of grass, but you will probably know it when you see it.

When you set your club down behind the ball, the blades of grass should reach up beyond the middle of the clubface. If they are much shorter than that, there probably isn't enough grass to catch too much of a flyer. On the other hand, if they are longer than that, you will lose too much speed through impact to worry about a flyer taking place. This type of rough doesn't look particularly daunting when you are getting ready to hit your shots, but the possibility of a flyer should have your full attention.

**Grass behind the ball.** In order to catch a flyer, there will need to be some grass behind the golf ball at impact. It is these blades of grass that are going to be responsible for your shot coming out with very little spin. If there happens to be a bare patch behind your ball with very little grass, you can probably get away without hitting a flyer. When grass is trapped between the ball and the clubface at impact, friction is reduced and spin rate drops significantly. It is these kinds of shots that come out flat and wind up sailing well beyond their intended target.

**Distance matters as well.** When trying to determine whether or not you are at risk of hitting a flyer, you should take the distance of the shot into account. The biggest risk is when playing shots from a distance that requires the use of your middle irons. Generally, the most common situation for a flyer to result is when hitting something between a six iron and nine iron into the green. It is possible to hit flyers with other clubs, but they are less common.

With short irons, you will have so much height on the shot that the flyer might not do that much damage – the shot may wind up a little long, but it shouldn't be too bad. On the other end, long iron shots don't have tremendously high spin rates anyway, so the difference here is often negligible. It is when you are going to play a middle iron and you think you have a flyer lie that you really need to be concerned.

**Think about the conditions.** You may be surprised to know that weather conditions can impact flyer lies as well. Specifically, you will be more likely to catch a flyer when you are playing on a wet day. When the grass is wet – as a result of rain, or even morning dew – there will be less friction present for the meeting of the ball and the clubface. Spin rates can be reduced even further in this case, and the flyer outcome will be very possible.

It takes an experienced eye to spot a flyer lie. However, now that you know what to watch for, you will be able to start seeing them more and more often even without much experience behind you. Pay attention anytime you walk into the rough and carefully examine the turf around your ball before planning your shot. There might not be anything you can do to gain total control over this kind of shot, but you can at least make a plan which will limit the damage that this lie can do.

## Making a Few Physical Adjustments

Once you have decided that you are dealing with a potential flyer lie, you will want to make a few adjustments to your swing technique. These changes aren't going to be anything particularly drastic, but they will be enough to impact the final result of the shot. Even though you won't have flyer conditions on the driving range, you should still practice these swing changes on the range just to make sure you are comfortable with them when the situation arises on the course.

The following three points are the key physical adjustments you should make when a flyer is a possibility.

**Choke down on the grip.** It probably seems like you are told to choke down on the grip of the club anytime your ball is in a difficult spot – and that is true, for the most part. By choking down on the grip, you will increase your control over the club during the swing. That means you are more likely to make solid contact, and making good contact can help you get as much spin as is possible from this lie.

Another benefit of choking down on the grip is the fact that you are going to lose a little swing speed along the way. If you do happen to catch a flyer, the decrease in your swing speed will help prevent the ball from going too far beyond the target.

**Play the ball slightly forward in your stance.** Many golfers move the ball back in their stance when they stray into the rough. That might work in some situations, but it would be the wrong move here. Moving the ball back in your stance will cause the shot to come out even lower, and that is not what you want to have happened in this case.

By moving the ball up, you should be able to pick up a little bit of launch angle, which will help to keep this shot under control. You probably won't gain any spin this way, but the higher launch should take a bit of distance off the ball and cause it to stop quicker as well.

**Open the face at address.** This is a bit of a 'pro move', but it is one which just about any amateur should be able to try. When you set up to the ball, open the face of your club just slightly. Then, make your swing as usual. With the face open, the ball should come out a little higher than it would otherwise.

Also, you might be able to squeeze out a little extra spin by using this technique. Don't worry about the open face leading to a slice, or even a fade. Most likely, when coming out of this kind of lie, the ball will fly almost perfectly straight.

That's it – by choking down on the grip, playing the ball forward in your stance, and opening the face of the club, you can do your best to minimize the effect of the flyer lie. This doesn't mean that the flyer is no longer a problem, it just might not be as big of a problem as it was before.

Using these adjustments should take extreme results out of play. In other words, instead of a shot that flies way over the green and into trouble, you might only miss your intended distance by a small amount. Still not an ideal result, but better than it could have been.

## Making Mental Adjustments

The adjustments you make on the mental side of the game might be even more important than the physical adjustments we outlined above. By making smart decisions, you can again mitigate the damage that will be done by a flyer lie. Golf is a game of decisions, and the more good ones you make during the course of a given round, the better off you will be.

So what can you do from a decision-making standpoint to improve your chances when it comes to a flyer lie? The following tips should help.

**Use one less club.** This should be an automatic reaction to finding that you have a possible flyer lie in the rough. As soon as you see that the lie may lead to a flyer, take one less club than you would have used for the yardage otherwise. By clubbing down, you will counteract some of the likely distance gain that you will experience from the lie.

The only exception to this rule is when you are playing over some kind of hazard. If you need the ball to at least carry a certain distance to stay out of trouble, you might want to stick with the original club. Using less club not only causes the shot to travel a shorter distance, but it also gives you more loft and a higher trajectory to work with.

**Consider laying up.** This might sound like a bit of a radical notion, but sometimes taking a chance on a flyer lie simply isn't worth the risk. For example, imagine you are playing a shot to a green that has a deep bunker guarding the back of the putting surface.

If your ball carries too far, or even lands on the green but bounces into the bunker, you will be facing a nearly impossible shot. Why even take the chance in this situation? You will be better served to lay up with your current shot, avoid the flyer altogether, and do your best to hit the next one close.

This strategy will take the big number out of play, and you might even still be able to save par. It will require patience to lay up when you can easily reach the green, but doing so might end up being in your best interest when all is said and done.

**Play to the biggest possible target.** When you have to hit a shot from a flyer lie, you are going to have a limited amount of control over the ball. Knowing that you should always be giving yourself the most margin for error that you can find. So, if you are going for the green, aim at the big part of the green where your ball will have the most room to roam.

It would be a mistake to aim over at a small corner of the putting surface just because that's where the pin happens to be located. You aren't worried about the pin right now – and you certainly shouldn't be worried about making a birdie. The goal is a par in this type of situation, and the best way to find that par is to put the odds in your favor. Play this shot as safe as you can and move on.

Patience is the name of the game when it comes to dealing with a flyer lie. If you wanted to be more aggressive with your approach shot, you should have hit your tee shot in the fairway. Now that you find yourself in the rough dealing with a possible flyer, you need to calm yourself down, think rationally, and play a safe shot.

Your round can easily get away from you if you decide to be aggressive out of this flyer lie in an attempt to still make a birdie. Don't let one bad decision ruin the rest of your round. Be smart, be patient, and use what you have learned to complete the hole as successfully as possible.

## Flyers in the Short Game

No golf instruction discussion would be complete without covering the short game. The short game tends to be overlooked too often, despite the fact that it is incredibly important to the score you wind up writing on your card at the end of the day. Since you can draw a flyer around the greens just like you can back in the rough along the fairway, it is important to touch on this topic before we conclude.

The first thing you need to know about flyer lies in the short game is that they look exactly the same as what we described earlier. If you have learned how to spot a flyer for your full swing, you already know how to spot one in the short game. Anytime you find your ball in the medium rough around the green, take a careful look at the lie to decide if you think it might be a flyer.

When you do think you have a flyer lie around the greens, you should plan on the ball coming out quickly and taking a big bounce when it lands. You probably won't hit the ball all the way over the green like you might from farther back – these are smaller swings and shorter shots, after all – but you could still hit the ball well beyond the target.

Adjust the size of your swing to account for the fact that you think the ball is going to come out quickly, and change your intended landing spot as well. There will always be an element of guesswork involved in this kind of shot, but you should get better and better at it as time moves along.

If at all possible, you should try to play lower chip and pitch shots when you think you have a flyer lie. Since the low bump-and-run type of shots doesn't use spin to stop the ball anyway, there won't be much difference between this shot and one hit from a good lie. You will already be planning on a big bounce and plenty of roll-out, so you might as well use a shot that plays right into that style.

Should you find that you have to play a downhill chip shot from a possible flyer lie, you may want to consider turning to a flop shot in order to give yourself a chance to stop the ball. If you hit a regular chip with a somewhat flat trajectory, it will be hard to get the ball to stop until it rolls off the green on the other side. By opting for the flop, you can put plenty of air under the ball and hopefully bring it down softly. This is still going to be a very difficult shot to pull off, but it might be your only real option.

Flyer lies are no fun. They actually don't look that scary when you encounter one on the course, since you can see most of the ball at address and you should be able to hit the shot far enough with ease. The devil is in the details, however. You won't have enough spin on the ball to control it properly, and it will be nearly impossible to guess accurately on your distance. Use the advice offered throughout this chapter to improve the way you deal with these kinds of shots when they arise.

# CHAPTER 20: THREE-QUARTER WEDGE

**M**ost avid golfers carry a pitching wedge and a gap wedge, plus a sand and/or lob wedge. Because there's generally just 5-6° of loft separating each club from the next, there are no huge variations in shot distances from wedge to wedge.

But no matter how many wedges you carry, you're bound to face shots that fall in between. For example, say you hit a full gap wedge 105 yards and a full sand wedge 85, and you need a shot that carries 92 yards. Or maybe you have a club to fit the exact yardage, but a headwind makes the shot play a little longer.

That's when you need the "three-quarter" shot. Some amateurs misinterpret the term, thinking it involves swinging at three-quarters of your normal effort. This invariably causes them to slow down rather than accelerate approaching impact, resulting in fat or thin contact.

In fact, the three-quarter shot requires the same power but a shorter swing – 75% (or so) of your usual length. Here's a simple method for playing the three-quarter wedge:

Address the ball with your standard wedge stance, placing the ball in the center.

Grip down a bit on the club and put a little extra weight on your left (lead) leg, which will lean the shaft toward the target.

Make your normal swing, focusing on a full backswing turn and a follow-through of the same length.

There's no need to consciously shorten your swing; gripping down on the club and pressing on your lead foot will take care of that. When practicing, vary the amount you grip down to determine how much difference a slight adjustment makes. And hit each wedge with different lengths on the driving range, because developing feel is key to success on in-between shots.

## Knock It Close with the Three Quarter Wedge

Amateur golfers love to talk about finding the 'secret' to golf. After all, the professionals make it look so easy that there must be one secret that can unlock great scores, right? Well, no. There is no secret to golf – playing well simply requires solid technique, good decision making, and plenty of practice.

There are no shortcuts to success in this game. All of the players you see excelling on TV each weekend have dedicated incredible amounts of time to honing their craft. They aren't there due to luck or chance – they have earned their spot through dedication and a belief in their own abilities.

While there is no secret that will allow amateurs to play like professionals, there are a few things that pro golfers do dramatically better than the average player. One of those things is hitting@ three quarter wedge shots. A 'three quarter' wedge is a term that is used to describe a shot played with a wedge from something less than a full distance.

So, for example, if you normally hit your sand wedge 100 yards in the air, you could use a three-quarter wedge when you are 70-80 yards from the target. Don't get too hung up on the exact definition of three quarter in terms of yardage – it is mostly just an expression to indicate a less-than-full swing wedge shot.

This is an important shot because you won't often find your ball lined up perfectly for a full swing wedge. You need to be able to hit your wedges close to the hole to set up a short birdie or par putts, but the course will rarely allow you to make a full swing from perfect yardage. More likely, you are going to have to get creative and use a variety of three-quarter wedge swings in order to set up your short putts.

Pro golfers are great at using soft swings to place the ball near the hole from inside 100 yards, but the average amateur golfer struggles mightily from this range. Taking the time to learn how to hit a three-quarter wedge would be a wise investment in the future of your game.

The natural instinct of many golfers is to swing as hard as possible all of the time. Most players pull a club from the bag with the intention of smashing the ball high into the air regardless of the situation. It should go without saying that this is a bad strategy, and it is one that will cost you strokes as the rounds go by.

If you are serious about becoming a better player, one of the first things you should learn to do is hit softer shots. By adding the ability to control the ball to your game, you will be better prepared to deal with a wider range of situations that you may face during a round. Also, learning how to make softer swings will help your feel for the swing as a whole, making it more likely that you will be able to solve problems when they come up.

All of the instruction below is based on a right-handed golfer. If you happen to play left-handed, please take a moment to reverse the directions as necessary.

*Tuning Down Your Full Swing*

You don't want to make an entirely new golf swing just to hit a three-quarter shot. Instead, you want to make your usual swing, with just a few adjustments to tune down the speed a bit. By slowing everything down through a variety of mechanical adjustments, you can effectively take 10 or 15 yards off of your shots without having to radically alter your mechanics. You have worked hard to create the swing you have now, so it would be a mistake to overhaul it completely just to hit some three-quarter wedges.

As you should already know, learning this kind of shot needs to happen first on the range before you try to take it onto the course. Using the following three adjustments during your next range session to work on learning the three-quarter wedge.

**Choke down on the grip.** The very first thing you need to do when learning the three-quarter wedge is to choke down on the grip of the club. By coming down the grip of your wedge by an inch or two you will be able to shorten your swing and limit the speed you generate.

Controlling your distance is all about controlling swing speed, and choking down on your wedges will put a limit on how much speed you build in the downswing. Not only will choking down on your wedges put a limit on your speed, but it will also help you keep the ball down lower to the ground, which is a great way to improve distance control effectively.

**Move the ball back in your stance.** Both of the goals of a three-quarter wedge – hitting the ball shorter and lower to the ground – will be served by moving the ball back in your stance. You don't need to move it way back in your stance, as just a couple of inches will make a big change in how the ball comes off the face of the club at impact.

If you normally play your full swing wedge shots from the center of your stance, try hitting your three-quarter wedges from a couple of inches behind that center point. As you practice, use a number of different ball positions until you are able to find one that gives you satisfactory results.

**Stand closer to the ball.** This point should come along with choking down on the grip, but some golfers fail to move in closer when they choke down. Since you are making the club effectively shorter as you choke down, you need to stand closer to the ball in order to promote solid contact.

Standing closer to the ball will also encourage an upright swing plane for this shot, which is perfect for driving the ball low toward the target with very little sidespin. Hitting a three-quarter wedge is all about accuracy and control, and standing slightly closer to the ball is going to help you with both of those things.

If you only make the three adjustments listed above, you will be well on your way to hitting beautiful three-quarter wedge shots. Of course, as you probably would guess, you are going to have to practice these adjustments before they become comfortable. The first few shots you hit with these adjustments in place might not be pretty but stick with it.

Your body and mind will adjust to the new positions that you have to reach in order to hit a good shot, and you will quickly start to see better and better results. It should only take two or three practice sessions before you begin to grow confidence in your ability to produce a nice three-quarter wedge shot on command.

## *Planning a Successful Shot*

The ability to execute a three quarter wedge swing is only part of the challenge – you also need to be able to plan the shot properly so that the ball will actually wind up close to the hole. If you fail to plan your shot, even the best swing in the world isn't going to do you a bit of good. Reading the terrain in front of you, getting accurate yardage, and checking on the hole location are just a few of the points that you have to keep in mind.

The planning of a quality three quarter wedge shot requires several steps, each of which is outlined below.

**Get two yardages.** Everyone on the course knows that you need to find the yardage to the hole before playing an approach shot – but that is only half of the equation. You need to know the number to the hole, but you also need to know the number that you have to carry to reach the green on your intended line. So, for example, on a wedge approach shot, you may have 100 yards to the hole, but only 85 to carry the ball onto the green.

Why does this second number matter? Since you will be bringing in your three quarter wedge shots lower than a full swing wedge, you have to know how far the ball needs to fly in the air in order to hit safely on the putting surface. If you are playing for a bounce up to the hole, you have to make sure that the ball is going to fly far enough to bounce on the green rather than getting stuck in the rough.

**Pick your club.** Now that you have both yardages in mind for the shot, you can decide which club you are going to pull from your bag. For this example, let's continue with the yardages of 100 to the hole and 85 to the front edge.

If you normally hit your sand wedge 95 yards, that isn't going to be enough club for the job – so you will have to go down to the pitching wedge. The pitching wedge, however, may fly around 115 with a full swing, meaning you will need to make a three-quarter swing to navigate this shot.

**Pick your line.** This is another point where many amateur golfers go wrong. It is tempting to simply aim directly at the hole and swing away, but that might not always be the best course of action. What if there is a bunker or pond lurking dangerously close to the hole?

It would be too risky to aim right at the hole, so in that case, you would want to aim away to the right or left in order to give yourself some margin for error. Also, if the green is severely sloped, you will want to aim toward the low side so you can play your next shot uphill instead of downhill. It requires patience to aim away from the hole with your three quarter wedge shots, but your scorecard will thank you in the end.

**Picture the shot.** Now that you have selected the club that you are going to use and the line you are going to take, the last step in this process is to actually picture the ball flying through the air toward the green. This is a vital step that many amateur golfers choose to skip. How high is the ball going to fly? Is it going to curve to the right or left? What it is going to do when it bounces?

The more detailed you are able to get with your visualization, the better chance you will have of executing the shot successfully when it leaves your club. It is a mistake to overlook the power of visualization in the game of golf, so be sure to give this last step in the process its just due.

At first, it might take you a bit of time to work through the four steps above. However, you should quickly get faster at making your way through this thought process as you gain experience and confidence. The majority of amateur golfers focus only on the actual swing when there is far more to playing good golf than just mechanics. Take the preparation for your shots just as seriously as you take the swing itself and you may be able to find improved success in time.

## The Role of the Golf Ball

Your equipment plays a role in your ability to hit three quarter golf shots as well. Certainly, you need a good wedge with plenty of grooves left in order to spin the ball up toward the target. Also, you need a good golf ball.

This is a point that is still overlooked by some players, and they pay the price when their shots don't come off as expected. You don't have to spend $50 per dozen to get a good ball, but you will probably need to invest a little bit of money if you want to hit great three-quarter wedge shots.

The issue comes down to spin. If you are using the cheapest golf ball off of the shelf – or worse, a ball you dug out of a pond – you aren't going to get the kind of spin necessary to stop your three quarter wedge shots properly.

The ball is going to be coming in lower than usual when you hit it with a three-quarter swing, meaning you will need a good spin rate to stop the ball after a reasonable distance. You are going to be playing for one or two bounces, but the ball should stop cold after those bounces. If you use a cheap or worn-out golf ball, it will likely bounce a couple of times and then continue to roll – meaning you will have almost no chance of stopping it near the target.

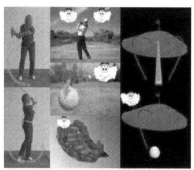

If you plan on playing three quarter wedge shots on a regular basis, you will want to pick out a golf ball that offers at least a moderate spin rate. The best way to judge the kind of spin you are going to get from a golf ball is simply to look at the retail price of that ball. Anything under $20 per dozen is highly unlikely to offer you a decent spin rate that will stop your wedge shots.

Balls over $40 are certainly going to have plenty of spin, but they will also be difficult for the average player to control off the tee. Therefore, the sweet spot for the average golfer is going to be golf balls that are sold for somewhere around $30 per dozen. Balls in this range tend to be soft enough to spin pretty well on your wedge shots without getting out of control on longer shots.

While the price range of a golf ball will give you a good indication of its capabilities, you also need to test the ball for yourself to see how it performs when coming off of your clubs. Try to buy sleeves of a few different ball brands that are in the right price range so you can test them out on the course.

Once you have played even just a few holes with a number of different golf balls, you will likely have no trouble at all deciding which one you like best. Sticking with one brand of ball for a long period of time is a good way to develop a feel and trust for the ball that will help you dial in your wedge shots nicely.

## Hit the Shot

One of the problems that is encountered by the average golfer who is trying to learn how to hit a three-quarter wedge is the tendency to 'give up' on the shot partway through the swing. Since they know that the club they are holding is capable of hitting the ball over the target, many golfers will slow up prior to impact in an effort to take the speed out of the swing. Obviously, this is the wrong way to go about the swing, and it is certain to lead to bad results.

Remember, the adjustments that you made before starting your swing were intended to take care of the distance problem, so you can just go ahead and swing the club. By choking down on the grip and moving the ball back in your stance, you will have effectively limited the club's ability to hit the ball its full distance – meaning your shot should come down somewhere near the target.

Of course, that doesn't mean you should go all out trying to smash the ball at impact. A controlled, balanced swing is the best way to go, just as it is around the rest of the course. Focus on maintaining a smooth speed throughout the swing, and don't let up as impact approaches.

One of the great things that will come along with experience in hitting three-quarter shots is the ability to feel certain distances. For example, after your ball has come to rest around 70 yards from the hole a few times, you will start to develop a natural feel for what kind of swing is required to hit the ball that distance.

This isn't something that you can analyze or even teach – it is just a natural development that will occur as you hit more and more three-quarter wedges. Regular practice of your partial wedge shots is important largely because that practice will allow you to develop your feel faster than if you only hit these types of shots out on the course.

Confidence is essential throughout all of golf, and the story is no different when you are hitting three-quarter wedges. Before you ever step up to take your stance, you already need to believe in your ability to pull off the shot. If you don't have that belief, you may as well pick a different kind of shot to put the ball on the green.

There is no faking it on the course – either you believe in yourself, or you don't. The best way to build confidence is by spending time working on various skills on the practice range. As you hit more and more three-quarter wedges on the range, your belief in this skill will naturally grow and you will look forward to the opportunity to show it off on the course.

Possessing the ability to hit quality three quarter wedge shots on command is something that can greatly help you in the pursuit of lower scores. You will find multiple opportunities in each and every round to hit three-quarter wedges, so this is a skill that you will get to show off on a regular basis. Build up your confidence on the range using the information contained above and you will be hitting it close out on the course before you know it.

Printed in Great Britain
by Amazon